Grades 3-4
Teacher Guide

Year Red, Semester 1

By Debbie Trafton O'Neal (Core)
and Karen Sanders (Bonus)

This teacher guide accompanies the Grades 3-4 Learner Resource and the Age 2–Grade 4 Teacher Class Kit.

Bible Backgrounds: Janet M. Corpus and Sarah S. Henrich
Editors: Arlene Flancher, Julie Bowe, and Elizabeth Drotning
Designer: Carl Nelson, Chance•Nelson & Associates
Illustrator: George Hamblin
Cover Photos: PhotoDisc

ISBN 0-8066-4712-4

www.augsburgfortress.org

Contents

Manufactured in U.S.A.
1 2 3 4 5 6 7 8 9 0 1 2 3 4 5 6 7 8 9

Introduction

Welcome to Witness!

Witness Sunday School Curriculum is a great way to teach the kids you know and care about how to "Learn from the Bible to Live the Good News." What is the good news? God promises, provides, and is present throughout human history. God the Father, Son, and Spirit is for us and with us, wherever we are and whatever we do. God is also for others: in our homes, in our neighborhoods, in our churches, and all around the world. That is news worth sharing!

As God's children—young and old, teachers and learners—we are witnesses to God's action in the world. Our salvation story is a story of God's gifts of Word, faith, and service. Each of these gifts functions as both meaningful connection and joyful invitation. **Word** connects us with the biblical story and invites us to use our minds to learn, make good choices, and communicate with others. **Faith** connects us with God's family and invites us to explore and affirm our identity as the church. **Service** connects us with our sisters and brothers, using Jesus as our model, and invites us to act lovingly for them. In Witness, your learners will encounter many ways to witness to others through exploring how they can express their faith in daily life with family, friends, the broader community, and God's creation.

Sunday school teachers play a valuable role in the faith development of young children. Whether you're a teaching veteran or a first-time teacher, this teacher guide will provide what you need to plan and carry out lively, engaging, and meaningful Sunday school sessions for your learners. Witness is designed to support teachers as they prepare for teaching children! Keep reading to learn more about Witness Sunday School Curriculum.

How Should I Get to Know Witness?

First, read pages 2-5 carefully. Then leaf through the Core and Bonus sessions in this teacher guide. Take a look at the leaflets and stickers in the learner resource. Explore the posters, activity cards, and reproducible sheets in the teacher class kit. Listen to the audio CD in the teacher class kit. Get familiar with the abbreviations for the learner resource (LR), teacher guide (TG), and teacher class kit (TCK).

What's in the Teacher Guide?

The teacher guide contains everything you need to know to teach up to 20 Sunday school sessions this semester. In addition to these introductory pages, this teacher guide contains age-level information on page 5, step-by-step plans for teaching 15 Core sessions on pages 6-80, an introduction to Bonus sessions on page 81, step-by-step plans for teaching five Bonus sessions on pages 82-91, and reproducible learner pages for Bonus sessions on pages 92-96. The inside front cover lists the scope and sequence for this semester. A family letter is found on the inside back cover. Make copies of this letter to distribute to learners during the first Sunday school session of the semester.

What's in the Learner Resource?

The learner resource (LR) contains two pages of color stickers and 15 four-page color leaflets to be used during the 15 Core sessions. To reduce week-to-week preparation time, prepare the leaflets and stickers before the semester begins. Separate the nested leaflets and group them by session. Cut apart the stickers and store them by session in small, resealable bags. Use folders or an accordion file to keep the materials for each session separate. Since many session activities require you to show pictures and read directions from the leaflet, make sure you have your own leaflet each week.

What's in the Teacher Class Kit?

Witness teacher class kits (TCK) are terrific for both learners and teachers. They contain posters, activity cards, reproducible sheets, and an audio CD. Many TCK items were designed for use in specific sessions, but

some items support teaching and learning throughout the course. Hang the colorful posters in your class area. Some have a biblical theme and some are designed to help learners make connections with their lives. Use the activity cards to tell stories and teach Faith Traits. Copy reproducible sheets for each learner to use during storytelling, art activities, and games. Among the reproducible sheets in each kit are those used as learner resources for Bonus sessions. Play a track from the audio CD each week and enjoy the varied formats and clever approaches to the Bible stories, using both music and spoken word.

What Are Core Sessions and Bonus Sessions?

There are two types of Witness Sunday school sessions: Core and Bonus. Each semester, the teacher guide contains 15 Core sessions that follow the salvation story. During the first semester of each Witness year, most Core sessions are based on stories from the Old Testament. A few stories at the end of Semester 1 focus on New Testament stories. These stories help learners prepare for Advent and Christmas. During the second semester of each Witness year, all Core sessions have New Testament stories as their basis, most from the Gospels of Luke and Matthew.

Each teacher guide also contains five Bonus sessions for each semester. These sessions offer added variety and flexibility. Read more about the Bonus session format on page 81.

What Is the Format of Each Core Session?

Each Core session is five pages long and describes everything you need for a 60-minute Sunday school session. The first page contains a session-at-a-glance chart that lists estimated activity times, needed materials, and learner activities. Find the Bible Text, the Key Verse, and the kid-friendly Big Idea statement on this page to prepare for presenting the story.

On the second page you'll find the Bible Background, Learner Goals and Age-Level Connection to enrich your preparation. Look for the Teacher Prayer and Question for Reflection in the sidebar for additional support and encouragement. Learner Goals carry out the Witness theme and broaden both teachers' and learners' understanding of the story. These goals match the characteristics of a witness: someone who knows the Word, grows in faith, and shows service. These Learner Goals also carry through to home, because the back page of each leaflet provides ways for families to know, grow, and show. The third, fourth, and fifth pages of each session describe what happens during your time with learners. Two factoids in each session provide additional background about the Bible story. Information about the material you will need and any preparation you should do before class appear as M&P before each activity. Note that activity times on each page are suggestions; expand or shorten depending on your learners' interests, classroom characteristics, availability of materials, and other factors.

Ready for the Story provides ideas for greeting learners and giving them something to do as others arrive, introduces a part of the story through one or more of the senses, and involves all learners in movement. Sidebar items include Witness Words and Transition Tip. Post the Witness Words, teach them during class, include them in word games and puzzles, or use them in other creative ways. Transition Tips help you shift to Explore the Story and may involve movement, signals, or props.

Learners hear the Bible story during **Explore the Story.** Use the Bible art and storytelling script on the second page of the leaflet for Storytelling. After setting up and telling the story, follow the teacher guide's suggestions for discussing the Faith Trait. Sidebar items include Kid Connect and More Movement. Kid Connect helps you engage kids in conversations and activities that are connected to the story. Use the movement activity when learners would enjoy moving their bodies.

Live the Story helps learners apply the story to their own lives and offers ideas for sharing the story and witnessing to others. Creative activity options like Kids Create mean kids can take home original art to help remember the story. Sidebar items on this page include Witnesses in the World, Teacher Boost, and Great Goodbyes. Go Global! is a sidebar in Sessions 2, 6, 9, 12, and 15. Before Session 2 copy Reproducible Sheets S and T (TCK), back to back, for each child. Plan how to use the puzzle with each activity.

Note: Most sidebar items (More Movement, Transition Tip, Witnesses in the World, Go Global!, and Great Goodbyes) contain activity suggestions. Because these activities are optional, materials and preparation are not found in the session-at-a-glance chart. Read ahead and plan accordingly!

What Is FAITH Traits?

Faith Traits is an exciting part of Witness that teach faith-based character and values to kids. Each session relates one Faith Trait to a Bible character and provides one or more activities that develop the trait in learners during the

ible to Live the Good News

Sunday school session and at home. With the inspiration of Bible characters, the guidance of the Spirit, and the support of others in their faith community, Faith Traits strengthen kids to be disciples.

Witness teaches 24 Faith Traits that stem from God's Graces of love, trust, courage, and hope. Love manifests itself as the Faith Traits of generosity, kindness, humility, compassion, empathy, respect, and thankfulness. Trust appears as the Faith Traits of cooperation, loyalty, obedience, boldness, and reverence. Courage shows itself as the Faith Traits of responsibility, self-discipline, perseverance, forgiveness, justice, honesty, and wisdom. Hope shines forth as the Faith Traits of harmony, stewardship, patience, peace, and joy.

Several items in the teacher class kit will help you teach Faith Traits and each session leaflet will include the Faith Trait as well.

How Should I Get Ready for Sunday School?

Find out all you can about your learners—especially what children that age enjoy and how they like to learn. Plan how you will *prepare yourself* to teach each week. Focus on what God's good news means for your life and your learners' lives.

Stock your classroom with basic supplies like paper, markers or crayons, scissors, glue sticks, and tape. Use adhesive putty, tape, or pushpins to display posters from the teacher class kit. Some posters are designed for use during specific sessions; others can be displayed for the entire semester. Make copies of the reproducible pages (TG) and sheets (TCK) as you need so that you have the correct number. The more you do ahead of time, the more time you will have to chat with kids as they arrive.

What Kind of Space Do I Need to Teach Witness?

Witness sessions can be used in a traditional classroom space with a table and chairs. Many activities encourage the use of comfortable spaces for storytelling and open spaces for movement. Pillows, beanbags, and other soft seating arrangements encourage learners to relax and enjoy stories. Carpet squares give each child a defined space when sitting in rows or a circle. When playing games that involve lots of movement, remove obstacles to make sure your learning space is safe.

How Can I Connect with My Learners?

Develop a warm relationship with each learner to build a positive foundation for learning and teaching in your Sunday school group. Use these tips throughout the semester to connect with your learners and help them feel important and valued in the group and loved by God.

- Learn each child's name and use names often during each session. Name tags help, especially when class sizes are larger or when some learners do not attend regularly.
- Welcome each child each week. Sit or kneel so you are at eye-level. Ask questions about activities, pets, family members, and other people and things important to kids.
- Encourage peer relationships! Use name tags and play name games to help learners remember their peers' names. Plan cooperative activities so everyone works toward one goal. Pay attention to how learners connect with each other in pairs, small groups, and all-boy or all-girl groups, and use the groupings that work.
- Provide alternative ways to participate when activities ask for hugging, since some kids are uncomfortable with this type of touching. Handshakes, high fives, and pats on the shoulder may be preferred.
- Ask learners to help with group tasks such as passing out leaflets, pressing the CD player button to start a song, and collecting art materials. Offer enthusiastic and genuine thanks for their help.
- Use the SOS (Some Other Stuff) activities on Reproducible Sheet H (TCK) when you have extra time in the classroom.
- Create consistency in Sunday school sessions so learners know when activities begin and end. You might use a chime or bell to signal a change to the next activity, or flip the lights on and off.
- Pray for your learners and the teaching ministry in your congregation.

Learn from the Bible to Li

A Final Word

As a Sunday school teacher, you share the Word, express your faith, and serve God and others. At Augsburg Fortress, Publishers, everyone involved in the writing and production of Witness sincerely hopes that these materials meet your teaching needs and help you and your learners travel further on your faith journeys. God bless you and your learners!

Age-Level Characteristics

Nurturing faith in Sunday school involves building relationships and understanding kids. Age is one of the biggest factors in determining how kids will learn and act. Here are some general traits of 3rd and 4th grade learners, some ideas for building relationships in your classroom, and a few tips for sharing God's Good News in kid-friendly ways.

Third and fourth graders:

- are full of energy
- enjoy the social aspects of working in groups
- can work independently
- have a highly developed sense of fairness
- enjoy playing games
- are curious and creative
- can be judgmental about themselves and others
- are beginning to become technologically savvy
- are intrigued by new information
- emulate people they admire
- are developing a sense of humor
- like to share stories about themselves, their families, and their friends
- learn by asking questions and like making choices about what they will do
- are growing in empathy and awareness of the needs of other people
- may already have some exposure to media with a more mature content (computer games, music, movies, videos, television programs)
- vary in their ability to begin thinking abstractly, outside the concrete world
- vary in their physical development and interests

- may vary in their reading and writing skills

To nurture faith and build relationships with these kids:

- learn their names
- celebrate birthdays or baptismal anniversaries
- ask them about their lives each week
- listen actively and carefully
- provide a safe place for them to share their stories
- have fun together
- give them leadership opportunities
- celebrate their accomplishments
- value their perspectives
- let them know you are their friend
- share parts of your own faith journey

Use these strategies to facilitate the development of friendships between kids:

- play name games
- plan activities where kids can really talk with each other
- play cooperative "team" games
- incorporate a "check-in" time during each session when kids can comfortably talk about what's happening in their lives (high points and low points of the week, favorite pet, favorite sport, best movie, and so forth)
- tailor activities so they're comfortable for all kids. Be sensitive to the variability in kids' willingness to interact with kids of the opposite sex.

To help them learn from the Bible to live the good news:

- play games to help them become comfortable finding their way around the Bible (books, chapters, and verses)
- ask them to share their opinions about the specific actions of a character in the Bible story
- invite them to imagine what a Bible story would be like if it happened now
- encourage them to dramatize an aspect of the story
- explore many aspects of a Bible story with a wide variety of activities that use different types of skills and abilities (cooking, going outside, playing games, doing a treasure hunt, solving puzzles, and so forth)
- provide opportunities for them to share Bible stories with younger children
- be "Witnesses in the World," and do service projects that will benefit kids and others in your congregation, community, and the world

The Beginning of the World

Bible Text

Genesis 1; 2:1-3

Key Verse

God saw everything that he had made, and indeed, it was very good. Genesis 1:31

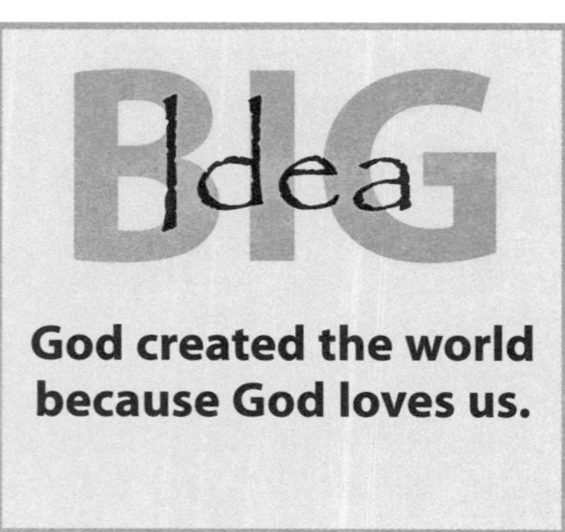

LR = Learner Resource
TCK = Teacher Class Kit
M&P = Materials and Preparation

Session at a Glance	What You Need	What Learners Do
Ready for the Story (15 minutes)		
Welcome the Witnesses	• Poster B and Witness CD (TCK), CD player, construction paper strips, crayons or markers, transparent tape	• Make nametag armbands.
Story Warm-Up	• Posters D and P (TCK), Reproducible Sheets A and B (TCK), Activity Card A (TCK), Faith Trait stickers (LR)	• Assemble Little Book of Faith Traits.
Story Fire-Up	• Poster A and Witness CD (TCK), CD player, mural paper, markers, tape or reusable adhesive putty	• Listen to nature sounds and make a creation mural.
Explore the Story (20 minutes)		
Story Set-Up	• Leaflet 1 (LR), crayons or markers	• Complete a coded creation puzzle.
Storytelling	• Poster E and Witness CD (TCK), Leaflet 1 and stickers (LR), CD player, Bibles, crayons, markers	• Locate and read the Bible story about creation.
Story Follow-Up	• Reproducible Sheet E (TCK), chalkboard and chalk or chart paper and marker	• Complete a Secret Animal Square activity and talk about thanksgiving.
Live the Story (25 minutes)		
Ways to Witness	• What you need: Leaflet 1 (LR), pencils	• Solve a Bible code and write a favorite verse in code.
Kids Create	• 12" x 12" (30 cm x 30 cm) squares of construction paper, fabric or paper scraps, glue, fine-tipped black markers • 2" x 12" (6 cm x 30 cm) poster board strips, construction paper, buttons	• Make a Creation Quilt Square or a Button Flower Bookmark.
Wrapping It Up	• Leaflet 1 (LR), Family Letter (TG, inside back cover)	• Review the Bible story and Witness Words. Pray together.

Bible Background

What Factors Shaped This Story?

Genesis is a poetic expression of belief that God created the world for good, for joy, and for interdependent relationships. The date and author of this writing are hidden in the long, rich history of Israel's life with God. The message is not intended to provide a scientific explanation of how creation happened or how everything works. Rather, the message speaks powerfully of the who and why of creation—celebrating God's good action on behalf of this world, our home.

What Is This Story About?

Genesis praises God's creation. Creation is the awesome home for all of the works of God's hands, including people, designed for their well-being. Genesis also is full of thanksgiving. Not only has God created all of this intricate beauty, but God has created us, too, as remarkable, wonderful creatures. Humans are called to be in charge of God's creatures. God has given us a remarkable vocation: to be stewards, partners with God in the ongoing preservation of creation. In those roles we participate in what sustains, blesses, and increases the glory of God's handiwork. The command "Love your neighbor" is about taking such good care that all of God's creatures flourish.

Why Is This Story Important?

The story of creation reminds us with whom and through whom we begin. A measure of the joy that creation inspires in us comes from knowing that its beauty has a source far beyond us. Its size, its complexities, and its interconnections leave us awestruck. The power of God's creating word challenges both our hearts and our minds to recognize the wonder of human beings as well. At their best these final creations show signs of the love and strength that God wills for all of life. Can we rise to the challenge of living in accordance with God's will?

Age-Level Connection

The story of creation may be familiar to the children you teach. They, too, are part of God's creation, with varied gifts, talents, and challenges. They are eager to learn about God's world, and are observant of the little things—an inchworm on a blade of grass, or a weed growing out of a sidewalk crack. Take time to listen to and learn from them!

Teacher Prayer

Thank you, God, for your beautiful creation! We are so blessed to enjoy the seasons, all kinds of weather, the mountains, trees, oceans, and deserts! Thank you, too, for the love you shower on us. Guide my thoughts and words today as I share your love with these learners. Amen

Question for Reflection

How do you show thanksgiving to God, even in the midst of the everyday things of life?

Learner Goals

KNOW
the story of creation

GROW
in their understanding of thanksgiving for all God gives

SHOW
concern for God's creation and a desire to be stewards of this great gift

FACTOID

The Jewish day began at sundown, so a full day was measured from evening to evening.

Ready for the Story (15 minutes)

Witness WORDS

creation, thanksgiving, stewardship

Welcome the Witnesses

M&P *Make a sample armband nametag with your name and symbols or words that represent your personality and interests. Display Poster B (Teacher Class Kit) where it can be viewed for the entire semester, if possible. Have Track 17 of the Witness CD (TCK) playing as the learners arrive. Have construction paper strips, crayons or markers, and transparent tape available.*

Greet the learners and show them your armband nametag. Invite them to make their own with words, pictures, and symbols that describe who they are. As they work, note that even though we are different, we are all created by God. Look at Poster B and ask learners to note similarities and differences between themselves and the Bible children illustrated there. Emphasize that God's love is for all people in all times and places.

Story Warm-Up

M&P *Make copies of Reproducible Sheets A and B (TCK). Prepare a sample Little Book of Faith Traits. Make additional copies of the booklet to have on hand for newcomers and guests. Display Posters D and P (TCK). Have the Faith Trait stickers (Learner Resource) and Activity Card A (TCK) available. Consider keeping each learner's Little Book of Faith Traits and corresponding stickers in a resealable bag to be used each session.*

Show learners a sample Little Book of Faith Traits. Distribute copies of the reproducible sheets. Demonstrate how to cut and fold the sheets to make a booklet. Tell the group that Faith Traits remind us of how we live as witnesses in God's world. Point to today's Faith Trait on Poster D (*generosity*). **God shows generosity to all people and calls us to do the same.** Have learners place today's Faith Trait sticker on its corresponding page inside their booklet. Each week they will add a new sticker to a page. Next, have a volunteer place today's marker from Activity Card A in the space provided on Poster P. Point to the poster and say today's Faith Trait together (*generosity*). Tell learners they will add new Faith Trait markers to the poster each time you meet. Make sure the learners write their names on their booklets. Collect and save them for next time.

FACTOID

Ancient people feared the darkness and welcomed each new day as a reminder of God's victory over the dark chaos at creation.

Story Fire-Up

M&P *Display Poster A (TCK). Have the Witness CD (TCK), a CD player, markers, tape or reusable adhesive putty available. Cut a large sheet of mural paper.*

Have the learners gather on the floor and look at Poster A. Draw attention to the lush creation scene. Then have learners close their eyes. Play Track 17 of the Witness CD and ask the learners to identify the nature sounds. Then have everyone open their eyes and gather at the mural paper. Give them time to work together, creating a nature or creation scene. Display the completed mural in the classroom or hallway. **Let's learn more about God's creation of the world and everything in it!**

Transition Tip

Have learners who were born in a particular month distribute materials and supplies, including writing tools and Bibles as needed.

Explore the Story (20 minutes)

Story Set-Up

M&P *Have Leaflet 1 (LR), crayons or markers ready.*
Ask learners to look at page 1 of their leaflets. Read the title and then give the learners time to color the coded puzzle. As they work, talk about some of the unique natural surroundings in your area. Ask learners to share their favorite outdoor places. Don't forget to mention a visit to a zoo, where a variety of God's creatures live! **God created a wonderful world because God loves us!**

Storytelling

M&P *Display Poster E (TCK) where it can be viewed for the entire semester, if possible. Have the Witness CD (TCK) available. Locate Leaflet 1 stickers (LR) for the Bible story activity. Have a CD player, Bibles, crayons, and markers available.*
Turn to page 2 of the leaflet. Ask a volunteer to read today's Bible Text, Big Idea, and Key Verse. Have a learner point to today's Big Idea on Poster E. Ask the learners to open their Bibles to the book of Genesis, the first book in the Old Testament. Let partners locate the Key Verse (Genesis 1:31) and read it together. Read it aloud again, all together. Find and read the Bible verses indicated on page 2 of the leaflet. If your group has little or no Bible experience, help them locate each listed verse and follow along as you read aloud. If they have some Bible experience, ask volunteers to locate and then read the verses aloud while the others follow along. After the reading is complete, distribute stickers, crayons, and markers and invite learners to complete the creation scenes on page 2. While they work, enjoy listening to "Creation Bounce" on Track 1 of the Witness CD.

Story Follow-Up

M&P *Make copies of Reproducible Sheet E (TCK). Have a chalkboard and chalk or chart paper and marker available.*
God created everything in the world, from the tiniest flea to the largest mammal—the blue whale! Have a volunteer distribute copies of the reproducible sheet and have fun with the activity. As learners work, talk about *thanksgiving* and how we show God we are thankful. Write the phrase "Thanksgiving is…" in large letters on a chalkboard or chart paper and add the learners' ideas and thoughts about the phrase in a list format. *(Being happy with what we have, praising God.)* **How do we show thanksgiving to others?** *(With hugs, by helping, through prayer.)*

Kid Connect

Display Poster F (TCK). **How can we care for creation?** Share ideas and then have partners complete "Taking Care of God's Earth" on page 3 of Leaflet 1 (LR).

More Movement

If weather permits, go for a walk and observe signs of God's creation. Challenge learners to observe, but not collect: something small, big, colorful, camouflaged, new today, and many years old.

Live the Story (25 minutes)

Ways to Witness

M&P *Have Leaflet 1 (LR) and pencils available.*

Have learners work through "Crack the Code!" on page 3 of the leaflet. It will be helpful if they first write out the alphabet and number each letter 1-26. After completing the activity, encourage each learner to write a favorite Bible verse or another affirming message such as "God loves you!" in code and see if a friend can crack it!

Teacher Boost

What an awesome thing to think about—the job of creating the world! If you ever feel discouraged in your own creative endeavors, remember that God created you, and you reflect God's image!

Kids Create (Choose one!)

M&P *For Creation Quilt Square: Have one 12" x 12" (30 cm x 30 cm) construction paper square per learner, pencils, glue, fabric or construction paper scraps, scissors, and black fine-tipped pens. Make a paper banner that reads, "Celebrate God's World!" For Button Flower Bookmark: Have one 2" x 12" (6 cm x 30 cm) strip of poster board per learner, paper scraps, scissors, and an assortment of buttons. Make a sample of the project you choose.*

Creation Quilt Square: Show learners a sample quilt square. Have them lightly sketch a creation or nature scene on their square with pencil, then cut fabric or paper scraps to fit the design, gluing them down. (As an alternative, divide the creation story into parts so that each learner designs one part on his or her square. When the squares are displayed together they will retell the story.) Demonstrate how to use a fine-tipped marker to make "stitching" lines around each square. Display the completed quilt squares under a "Celebrate God's World!" banner.

Button Flower Bookmark: Show the learners a sample bookmark. Give each learner a poster board strip. Show them how to cut or tear flower petals and leaf shapes from scrap paper. Assemble and glue the flower designs on one end of the strip, then glue one or more buttons to the center of the flower. Have learners add their name or today's Key Verse to the bookmark.

Witnesses in the World

Find out how your church practices good earth stewardship. Do you recycle worship folders and other paper? Collect aluminum cans? Use porcelain mugs rather than paper cups? Share the information with the learners and invite their additional ideas for making your church earth-friendly!

Wrapping It Up

M&P *Have Leaflet 1 (LR) and copies of the Family Letter from the inside back cover of the Teacher Guide available.*

Turn to page 4 in the learner leaflet. Each week this page will include activities for families to do together. Talk about the Witness Words that appear on this page. Help learners define them and then tell how they relate to today's Bible story. Make sure the learners collect their leaflets, Bibles, and completed projects to take home. Give each learner a copy of the Family Letter. Ask them to join you in prayer: **Dear God, thank you for bringing us together! Thank you for creating the world and everything in it. Help us learn to be good caretakers of your creation. Amen**

GREAT good byes

As the learners leave, emphasize that God created everything good because God loves us. Encourage them to make *thanksgiving* and *stewardship* daily practices.

Living With God's Promise

Session at a Glance	What You Need	What Learners Do
Ready for the Story (15 minutes)		
Welcome the Witnesses	• Large construction paper rainbow cut into jigsaw puzzle pieces, transparent tape or thumbtacks	• Assemble a rainbow puzzle.
Story Warm-Up	• Posters D, E and P (TCK), Activity Card A (TCK), Little Book of Faith Traits, Faith Trait stickers (LR)	• Discuss rainbows and today's Faith Trait.
Story Fire-Up	• Red, yellow, and blue ice cubes; clear plastic cups; chart paper graph; markers	• Predict color changes as ice cubes melt together.
Explore the Story (20 minutes)		
Story Set-Up	• Poster A (TCK), Leaflet 2 (LR)	• Complete an animal word search.
Storytelling	• Leaflet 2 (LR), Witness CD (TCK), CD player	• Hear the story of Noah and the ark.
Story Follow-Up	• Chalkboard and chalk or chart paper and marker	• Discuss the Bible story and the Faith Trait *obedience*.
Live the Story (25 minutes)		
Ways to Witness	• Leaflet 2 and stickers (LR)	• Discuss situations involving obedience.
Kids Create	• 8 medium-sized safety pins for each learner, seed beads in rainbow colors • White construction paper, 1" x 9" (2.5 cm x 23 cm) strips of construction paper in rainbow colors, scissors, glue sticks	• Make a Rainbow Bead Pin or Rainbow Weaving.
Wrapping It Up	• Leaflet 2 (LR)	• Review the Bible story and Witness Words. Pray together.

Bible Text

Genesis 6–9

Key Verse

I have set my bow in the clouds, and it shall be a sign of the covenant between me and the earth. Genesis 9:13

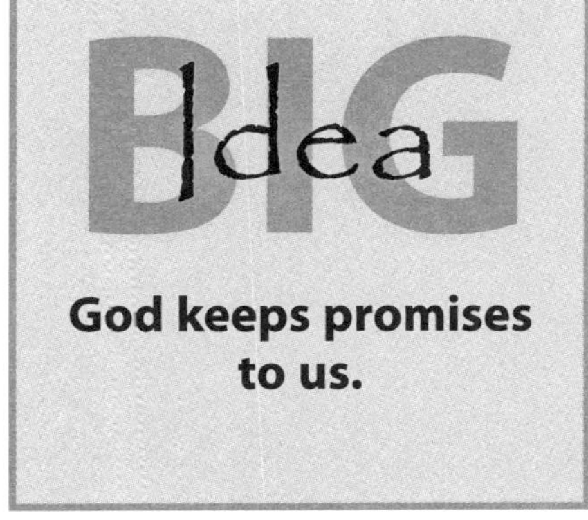

LR = Learner Resource
TCK = Teacher Class Kit
M&P = Materials and Preparation

Teacher Prayer

Thank you, loving God, for all you give us! In your wisdom you created the living earth with seasons and weather and growing things. But most of all, I thank you for always keeping your promises. Help me share your promises with these children today. Amen

Question for Reflection

How do the faithfulness and obedience of Noah and his family inspire you in your daily life?

Learner Goals

KNOW
the story of Noah and God's promise

GROW
in faith and understanding of obedience to God's word

SHOW
care and concern for God's living world

FACTOID

The ark would have been approximately the length of one-and-a-half football fields.

Bible Background

What Factors Shaped This Story?

This richly packed and important text is made up of two ancient traditions woven into three episodes. Each episode has its own themes (6:5—7:12; 7:13—8:19; 8:20—9:17), all of which turn around the pivotal verse 8:1. God had willed a creation ordered around stewardship and Sabbath rest, but creation resisted its creator and betrayed God's purposes. From 6:5—7:24 God is seriously grieved by the creation. The evil heart of humankind (6:5) troubles the heart of God (6:6). This text suggests that there is a painful crisis for God in God's dealings with creation. By the end of this passage there is a change in God, rather than in humankind, which gives the opportunity for a new beginning for creation itself.

What Is This Story About?

In this story, Noah will be a sign of future possibilities. He alone is not at odds with his creator. The turning point of the story comes in 8:1, where God "remembered Noah" and all the creatures with him. God's remembering leads to a new beginning for creation. Fresh from the ark, Noah worships God at a newly built altar. God speaks in his heart (8:21), the very place where God had been troubled. God makes a vow based on his own decision and character, for God recognized that the human heart has not changed and will not. Hope for creation can be based only on God's patient love. Humans will betray their creator, but God will and does still keep promises. This promise to sustain creation even when its creatures resist God's love is good news for Noah and for us.

Why Is This Story Important?

In 9:1-7 we hear again words from the first creation story. Humans remain in God's image. They are still to be fruitful. But now God is deeply aware of human weakness (8:21). Grace is God's willingness to try again with us. Everyone who is a loving parent, or had a loving parent, might understand the hope and vulnerability of love like God's. In Genesis, the creator of the cosmos expresses such love in the promise to never again destroy all of creation by flood. Christians see God's vulnerable love and God's power over destruction in the saving events of Jesus' death and resurrection.

Age-Level Connection

The story of Noah's obedience to God is filled with appealing images of an ark, animals, rain, and a beautiful rainbow. It is understandable why this Bible story is a favorite of young and old alike. The story's symbols and their meanings are a constant reminder of the grace God promises us.

Ready for the Story (15 minutes)

Welcome the Witnesses

M&P *Prepare a large rainbow from construction paper. Cut it into puzzle pieces. Have tape or thumbtacks available.*
Greet the learners as they arrive. If there are newcomers or guests, be sure to welcome them personally. Distribute puzzle pieces and work together to assemble the rainbow on a wall or bulletin board. Ask learners to tell about times they have seen rainbows. Have they made rainbows by spraying water? Or with prisms? Encourage everyone to share rainbow experiences!

Story Warm-Up

M&P *Display Posters D, E, and P (TCK). Locate Activity Card A (TCK). Have the learners' copies of the Little Book of Faith Traits (see Session 1 "Story Warm-Up") and Faith Trait stickers (Learner Resource) available.*
Point to the rainbow puzzle. **What are the colors of the rainbow?** *(Red, orange, yellow, green, blue, indigo, and violet.)* **What makes a rainbow?** *(Sunshine, rain/moisture.)* **What Bible story does the rainbow remind you of?** *(Noah and the ark.)* Read together today's Big Idea on Poster E. **Today we're going to learn more about Noah, the ark, and the rainbow—a sign that God keeps promises to us.** Refer to Poster D and review the faith trait from last time (*generosity*). Ask learners to tell when they experienced generosity during the past week. Then read together today's Faith Trait (*obedience*). Share examples of obedience with the learners. Then give them their copies of the Little Book of Faith Traits and Faith Trait stickers. Have them place today's sticker on its corresponding page. Ask a learner to place today's marker from Activity Card A on Poster P. Then collect the booklets and save them for next time.

Story Fire-Up

M&P *Ahead of time, freeze food coloring and water in ice cube trays, creating at least two red, two blue, and two yellow cubes. Have three clear plastic cups and a variety of markers available. Make and display a chart paper graph.*
Show the learners the colored ice cubes. Explain that red, yellow, and blue are called *primary colors*—the "building blocks" of all the rainbow colors. In separate cups, place red and yellow cubes, red and blue cubes, and yellow and blue cubes. Place the cups in a sunny or warm location. **What colors do you predict these ice cubes will melt into?** Have the learners use colored markers to make their predictions on the graph. Be sure to have an assortment of markers, not just the final colors (orange, purple, and green).

obedience, ark, covenant, rainbow

FACTOID

During the flood, not only did water fall from the sky as rain, it gushed out of the ground like a geyser!

Transition Tip

Ask volunteers to distribute classroom materials while you display the Session 2 posters. Consider placing the posters at the children's eye level rather than your own.

Explore the Story (20 minutes)

Third and fourth graders are capable of caring deeply for living things. Talk about specific ways to care for God's creation—the people, land, animals, and birds.

Play a game of Twister© or move outdoors for a game of "I Spy." Call out a color *(I spy red)*. Learners take turns guessing the location of the color. *(The flowers... the church roof...)* The one who guesses correctly begins the next round. As you play, emphasize that God makes all the colors!

Story Set-Up

M&P *Display Poster A (TCK). Distribute Leaflet 2 (LR) and pencils.* Have learners look at page 1 of the leaflet. Ask a volunteer to read the directions for "Can You Find...?" Compare the animals shown on Poster A to those listed in the leaflet activity. Have the learners work alone or in pairs to complete the activity. **Noah brought two of every kind of animal on the ark. Which of the animals listed here have you seen?** *(Accept all answers.)*

Storytelling

M&P *Have the Witness CD (TCK), Leaflet 2 (LR), a CD player, and pencils available.*

Read the Bible Text, Big Idea and Key Verse on page 2 of the leaflet. Play "Extreme Quarters!" (Track 2 of the Witness CD), listening to the story of Noah and the ark. Then refer to the story printed here as you help the learners complete "A Rainbow Promise" on page 2 of their leaflets:

God was pleased with Noah because Noah was walking with God. God wasn't happy with the people in the world who were disobeying God's plan. God told Noah to build an ark. "I am going to bring a flood to destroy the earth," God said. "But I will make a covenant or promise with you and your family. Bring two of every living creature with you. I will save them too." The rain poured from the sky. The flood continued for forty days and forty nights. But God remembered Noah and everyone on the ark. After the rain stopped, the water dried up from the earth. God told Noah to bring everyone out of the ark. Then Noah built an altar to worship God. God was pleased and said, "I will never send a flood to destroy the earth again." And God set a rainbow in the sky as a sign to remind people of God's covenant or promise.

Story Follow-Up

M&P *Have a chalkboard and chalk or chart paper and marker available.*

Bible stories help us understand how to live the life that God plans for us. In today's story, Noah was obedient to God's word. What does *obedience* mean? *(As learners respond, write their ideas on a chalkboard or chart paper. Help them understand that* obedience *is doing what we are told to do by those who love us or have our best interests in mind.)* **When God told Noah to build the ark, it wasn't even raining yet! But Noah trusted God's promise. When we are obedient to those who love us, we trust them to care for us.**

Live the Story (25 minutes)

Ways to Witness

M&P *Have Leaflet 2 and Session 2 stickers (LR) available.*
Have learners find "Follow the Rules" on page 3 of the leaflet. **God gives us rules and guidelines to live by. Noah's obedience is an example of the kind of life God wants us to live.** Ask volunteers to read aloud the stories about Miguel, Verlecia, and Hailey. **What might the characters do in each situation? What would you do? What makes your decision easy or difficult?** Give the learners time to share their thoughts and ideas with the class. Continue with "Rainbow Prayer." Read about rainbows together and give the learners time to create a rainbow prayer of their own, adding stickers to the page.

Kids Create

M&P *For Rainbow Bead Pin: Have available for each learner eight medium-sized safety pins and seed beads in rainbow colors (10 each of red, orange, yellow, green, blue, indigo/dark blue, and violet/purple). For Rainbow Weaving: Have white construction paper and construction paper strips in rainbow colors (1" x 9" (2.5 cm x 23 cm)) for each learner, scissors, and glue sticks. Make a sample of the project you choose.*
Rainbow Bead Pin: Show learners a completed project. Then help them thread the point of a safety pin through the circular ends of seven closed pins. Close the first pin. One at a time, open the seven pins and demonstrate how to slip 10 like-colored beads onto each pin. Close the pins. When complete the pins will resemble the bands of a rainbow. **We can wear our rainbow pins as a reminder that God keeps promises to us!**
Rainbow Weaving: Show learners how to fold a sheet of white construction paper in half, cutting it through the fold at 1" (2.5 cm) intervals, ending each cut approximately 2" (5 cm) from the end. Open the sheet and show them how to weave colorful strips of paper into a rainbow pattern. Glue and trim the ends. For a fun variation, have the learners prepare their white paper using "wavy" cuts, and then weave as usual. The finished product will provide an optically interesting design!

Wrapping It Up

M&P *Have Leaflet 2 (LR) available.*
Make sure the learners have their leaflets, Bibles, and completed projects to take home. Review the Bible story and the Witness Words that appear on page 4 of the leaflet. Have learners tell how the words relate to the Bible story. Look at the activities on page 4 and encourage the learners to try them with their families. Then ask the learners to join you in prayer: **Thank you, Creator, for sun and rain, for daytime and nighttime, for family and friends. Help us remember to trust and obey you each day! Amen**

Teacher Boost

Although your learners may have heard the Noah story many times, introducing new thoughts about it can help them begin to share their understanding through activities and discussion. Emphasize the promises that God makes and always keeps.

Witnesses in the World

Ask church leaders about places that your congregation supports when weather-related disasters occur. Bring pictures and information about one or more of these places. Talk with the learners about ways your class could help people experiencing droughts or floods.

Go Global!

Read the Go Global! activity on Reproducible Sheets S and T (TCK). See page 3.

GREAT good byes

Review the Key Bible Verse and encourage learners to look for rainbow images this week. Remind them that God always keeps promises to us!

Faithful People

Bible Text

Genesis 18:1-15; 21:1-7

Key Verse

Is anything too wonderful for the LORD? Genesis 18:14

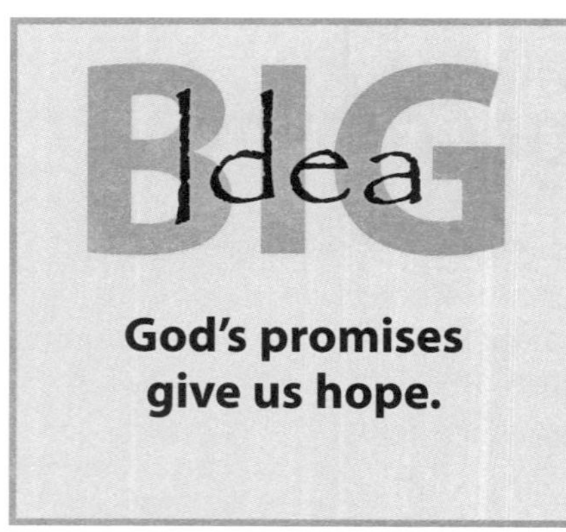

LR = Learner Resource
TCK = Teacher Class Kit
M&P = Materials and Preparation

Session at a Glance	What You Need	What Learners Do
Ready for the Story (15 minutes)		
Welcome the Witnesses	• Poster E and Witness CD (TCK), CD player	• Review Big Ideas.
Story Warm-Up	• Posters D and P (TCK), Activity Card A (TCK), Faith Trait stickers (LR), learners' copies of the Little Book of Faith Traits	• Review Faith Traits from Sessions 1 and 2, and learn the Faith Trait for today: *patience*.
Story Fire-Up	• A small portable tent or large blankets, table and chairs	• Set up a tent to use during the Bible story.
Explore the Story (20 minutes)		
Story Set-Up	• Leaflet 3 (LR), Bibles	• Learn about the symbol of stars and how they relate to the story of Abraham and Sarah.
Storytelling	• Leaflet 3 (LR), Bibles	• Complete missing portions of the Bible story.
Story Follow-Up	• Reproducible Sheets C and D (TCK), Witness CD (TCK), CD player, crayons or markers, scissors, transparent tape	• Make puppets to retell the Bible story.
Live the Story (25 minutes)		
Ways to Witness	• Leaflet 3 (LR), pencils	• Think about the promises we make to God.
Kids Create	• Leaflet 3 (LR), pocket pattern, blue construction paper, scissors, paper punch, transparent tape, 20" (50 cm) gold or yellow yarn strands, index cards • Star stencils/patterns, metallic paper, fine-tipped permanent markers, nylon filament thread (fishing line)	• Make a Promise Pocket or stars for a Star Walk.
Wrapping It Up	• Leaflet 3 (LR), reminder notes to bring a baby photograph next time	• Review the Bible story and Witness Words. Pray together.

Bible Background

What Factors Shaped This Story?

Genesis is about God's promise and God's faithfulness to that promise. It also is about how people respond in faith to God's call. People experience this call in the real circumstances of their lives, often in complex and difficult situations. Yet if there is to be a people Israel who will be a blessing to all nations, individuals must discover trust in God who wants and is able to keep those promises. Genesis closes on a note of confidence about God (Genesis 50:20, 24), but it is open-ended. This relationship between God and humans is on a rocky road into God's promised future.

What Is This Story About?

God makes a promise to Abraham in Genesis 12:1-3 and more fully declares it in 17:3-8. God insists that Abraham and Sarah will be parents of a vast number of descendants, even though they are too old for this to be possible. Both Abraham and Sarah have occasion to laugh at the absurdity of it all (17:17; 18:12). Yet they remain willing to receive unknown visitors. In Genesis 18 Abraham takes the lead, hurrying to see to the comfort of his guests, whoever they might be! What Abraham and Sarah receive from them lies at the heart of the passage (18:10, 14). The stranger promises the impossible and asks whether they believe that for God anything is impossible. Can they trust God's impossible promise? Because the stranger knows of Sarah's secret laugh, perhaps he knows other secrets as well, even the secret of God's plan and power.

Why Is This Story Important?

The challenge to trust God's ability to do the impossible in the lives of ordinary people is a recurrent theme in the Bible. It is a central question at the birth of Jesus, when Gabriel reassures Mary that God's promises will be kept. Jesus later tells his disciples that God makes possible the entry of even the most unlikely persons into God's kingdom. Praying in Gethsemane, Jesus gives us another example of trust as he turns his life over to God.

Age-Level Connection

Many learners may have younger brothers, sisters, and cousins, or perhaps are in a childcare situation where they are with younger children or babies. They can understand the excitement of having a new baby and that babies bring hope, while requiring patience! Appearing within this session is the Faith Trait *patience*. Abraham and Sarah exemplified this Faith Trait.

Teacher Prayer

Patient God, nothing is too wonderful for you! Sometimes I forget that in the busyness of life. Help me to always rejoice in the wonder of the life you give me. Amen

Question for Reflection

How has God surprised you?

Learner Goals

KNOW
the story of God's promises to Abraham and Sarah

GROW
to understand what it means to be God's faithful followers

SHOW
understanding of God's promises to them

FACTOID

In Hebrew, the word *Isaac* sounds like the word for "laugh."

Ready for the Story (15 minutes)

promise, faithful, descendant

Welcome the Witnesses

M&P *Display Poster E (Teacher Class Kit). Have songs from the Witness CD (TCK) playing as learners arrive.*

Welcome the learners by name and ask about their activities since the last time you met. When everyone has arrived, direct the group's attention to Poster E. Review and discuss the Big Ideas from Sessions 1 and 2. *(God created the world because God loves us. God keeps promises to us.)* Show them today's Big Idea *(God's promises give us hope)*.

Story Warm-Up

M&P *Display Posters D and P (TCK). Locate Activity Card A (TCK) and Faith Trait stickers (Learner Resource). Have the learners' copies of the Little Book of Faith Traits available (see Session 1 "Story Warm-Up").*

Ask a learner to point to the Faith Traits on Poster D that you have talked about so far (*generosity, obedience*). Ask learners to share examples of generosity or obedience they experienced in the past week. Then ask another learner to point to today's Faith Trait (*patience*). **When do you need to be especially patient?** *(When I'm waiting for my sister to get ready for school; when I'm hungry but Mom says I can't eat yet.)* **How can God help us be patient?** *(We can pray to God and ask for patience.)* Ask a volunteer to distribute the Little Book of Faith Traits and Faith Trait stickers. Have the learners place today's sticker on its corresponding page. Have a learner place today's marker from Activity Card A on Poster P. Collect and save the booklets for next time.

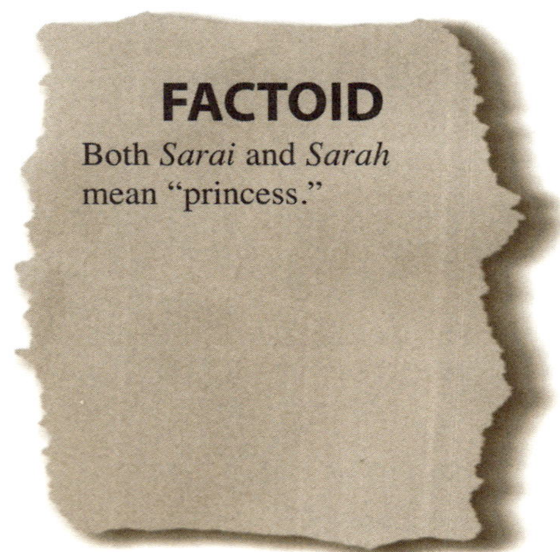

Story Fire-Up

M&P *If you have a small portable camping tent, bring it to class and make sure you are familiar with setting it up. If a tent is not available, or if your group is large, bring several large blankets that can be draped over tables and chairs to create a "tent."*

Ask the learners if they have ever been camping in a tent. Where did they go? Did they sleep on the ground? How did they cook their food? Talk about how living conditions during Bible times were quite different from the way the learners may live today. **Today's Bible story is about Abraham and Sarah. They lived in a very dry land. Their home was a tent because they traveled around with their herds of animals. Today I need your help setting up a tent!** Work together to set up a tent, reminding the learners to practice patience while you work!

Transition Tip

Sometimes a disruptive child is seeking attention. Find ways for him or her to receive positive attention before a disruption occurs. For example, ask this child to hold one end of a blanket as you make your tent.

Explore the Story (20 minutes)

Story Set-Up

M&P *Have Leaflet 3 (LR), pencils, and Bibles available.*
Gather together inside your tent. Distribute Leaflet 3 and pencils. Invite learners to look at page 1. Read the title and then give the learners time to complete the "What Is It?" activity. Talk about Christian symbols that the learners may know (a cross, ship, lamb, dove, fish, and so forth). Note the large star surrounded by many smaller stars on page 1, representing Abraham and his many descendants. **A *descendant* is someone who lives after a person. So we, and all followers of God, are descendants of Abraham.**

Storytelling

M&P *Have Leaflet 3 (LR), pencils, and Bibles available.*
Remain inside the tent as you show the learners the Bible Text, Big Idea, and Key Verse that appear on page 2 of the leaflet. Then have learners work in small groups to complete the Bible story found on page 2. *(Correct phrases to complete the story include: "saw three men standing near him;" "rest yourselves under the tree;" "bring a little bread;" "make ready quickly cakes;" "Where is your wife Sarah?" "There, in the tent;" "Sarah laughed to herself;" "Is anything too wonderful for the Lord?")* Take turns reading the completed story aloud. **Who had hope in this story?** *(Abraham and Sarah.)* **What did they hope for?** *(A child.)* **How would you complete this sentence? Sarah and Abraham were patient because…** *(Answers will vary.)*

Story Follow-Up

M&P *Make enough copies of Reproducible Sheets C and D (TCK) so that each learner will have a set of puppets. Locate the Witness CD (TCK) and a CD player. Have crayons or markers, scissors, and transparent tape available. If needed, move the group out of the tent to a table or open area to work.*
Have a volunteer distribute copies of the reproducible sheets. Give the learners time to color, cut out, and assemble their puppets. As they work, play Track 3, "How the Promise Comes," of the Witness CD. Encourage the learners to listen for the word *promise* in the song. Then remind them that God's promises give us hope. When the puppets are complete, let the learners use them to retell today's Bible story with a partner or in small groups. Encourage them to use the puppets to retell the story with their families at home.

Complete "The Promises of God" on page 3 of the learner leaflet, assigning one or two verses to each learner. *(Answers: anything, one another, reward you, call, answer, wish, answer, receive, answer, sin, spirit, near, ask, prayer, receive, rescues. Message: God answers prayer.)*

In today's Bible story, Sarah laughed because she thought she was too old to have a baby. Laughter is good medicine! Exercise your lungs by having a "laughing" contest. See who can laugh the longest, quietest, and silliest!

Teacher Boost

There will always be days when we worry and fret over things that we have little control over. It is then that we need to recall the words from Genesis 18:14—Is anything too wonderful for the Lord?

Witnesses in the World

As Christians, we live life filled with hope! Team up with other Sunday school classes to spread hope in your community and world. If your congregation participates in soap drives, quilting, or world hunger projects, find ways for your learners to get involved!

GREAT good byes

Ask learners to join you in saying today's Key Verse *(Is anything too wonderful for the Lord?)*. Remind them that God's promises give us hope and *patience*.

Live the Story (25 minutes)

Ways to Witness

M&P *Have Leaflet 3 (LR) and pencils available.*
Talk about the many promises that God makes to us. **What promises can we make to God?** To pray more? To read the Bible more? To invite someone to church? Have the learners find "My Promises to God" on page 3 of their leaflet and take a few moments to think about the promises they want to make to God. Then have them write their ideas in the space provided. If time permits, invite volunteers to share what they wrote.

Kids Create

M&P *For Promise Pocket: Make pocket patterns on paper (approximately 4.5" x 7" [11 cm x 18 cm]). Locate Leaflet 3 (LR), blue construction paper, scissors, paper punch, transparent tape, 20" (50 cm) gold or yellow yarn strands, index cards, and pencils. For Star Walk: Have available various sizes of star stencils/patterns, metallic paper (available at craft stores), pencils, fine-tipped permanent markers, scissors, transparent tape, and nylon filament thread (fishing line). Make a sample of the project you choose.*
Promise Pocket: Show learners a sample Promise Pocket. Have them trace two pocket patterns on blue construction paper. Cut out the pockets, place one on top of the other and punch holes around three sides at ⅓" (1 cm) intervals. Tape one end of a yarn strand to the back of the pocket, then sew the pieces together. Cut off excess yarn and tape the loose end to the back of the pocket. Have the learners choose several verses from "The Promises of God" puzzle on page 3 of the leaflet, write them on index cards, and place them inside their Promise Pocket. Encourage learners to keep their Promise Pocket in their Bible or share it with a friend!
Star Walk: Have learners trace and cut out stars from metallic paper. Consider making one star for every Sunday school child, or the entire congregation! Have learners write names on the stars. Suspend them from a hallway ceiling or fellowship area as a reminder that we are all descendants of Abraham and Sarah, and recipients of God's promises. If making stars for the congregation, include a note about the Star Walk in a worship bulletin or church newsletter explaining its symbolism.

Wrapping It Up

M&P *Have Leaflet 3 (LR) available. Write a note for learners to take home, reminding them to bring one of their baby photographs next time, if possible.*
Have learners collect their leaflets, Bibles, and projects to take home. Review the story of Abraham and Sarah. Talk about the Witness Words that appear on page 4 of the leaflet. Have the learners tell how the words relate to today's Bible story. Encourage learners to share the activities on page 4 with their families. Also, distribute notes and ask each learner to bring a baby photograph of himself or herself next time. Close with a prayer: **Dear God, thank you for bringing us together today. Help us remember the story of Abraham and Sarah, and your faithfulness to them. Help us live each day with patience and hope. Amen**

God Gives Us Courage

Session at a Glance	What You Need	What Learners Do
Ready for the Story (15 minutes)		
Welcome the Witnesses	• Poster E and Witness CD (TCK), CD player	• Hear a song about baby Moses and review Big Ideas.
Story Warm-Up	• Posters D and P (TCK), Activity Card A (TCK), Faith Trait stickers (LR), copies of the learners' Little Book of Faith Traits	• Review Faith Traits from Sessions 1-3, and learn the Faith Trait for today: *responsibility*.
Story Fire-Up	• Baby photographs of the learners	• Talk about babies and toddlers.
Explore the Story (20 minutes)		
Story Set-Up	• Poster B (TCK), blue carpeting, rug or blanket, doll or baby basket	• Talk about Bible times children.
Storytelling	• Leaflet 4 (LR), crayons or markers, Bibles	• Read the Bible story and answer questions.
Story Follow-Up	• Leaflet 4 (LR)	• Talk about the feelings of the Bible story characters.
Live the Story (25 minutes)		
Ways to Witness	• Slips of paper, basket	• Think of ways to show courage in the coming week.
Kids Create	• Sheets of construction paper, 1" (2.5 cm) wide strips of construction paper in a variety of colors, scissors, stapler, glue • Small picture frame matte boards or thin cardboard picture frames, old puzzle pieces, fast drying acrylic paint, paint brushes, and water	• Make a Woven Windsock or Puzzle Piece Picture Frame.
Wrapping It Up	• Poster C (TCK), Leaflet 4 (LR)	• Review the Bible story and Witness Words. Pray together.

Bible Text

Exodus 2:1-10

Key Verse

When the child grew up, she brought him to Pharaoh's daughter, and she took him as her son. She named him Moses, "because," she said, "I drew him out of the water." Exodus 2:10

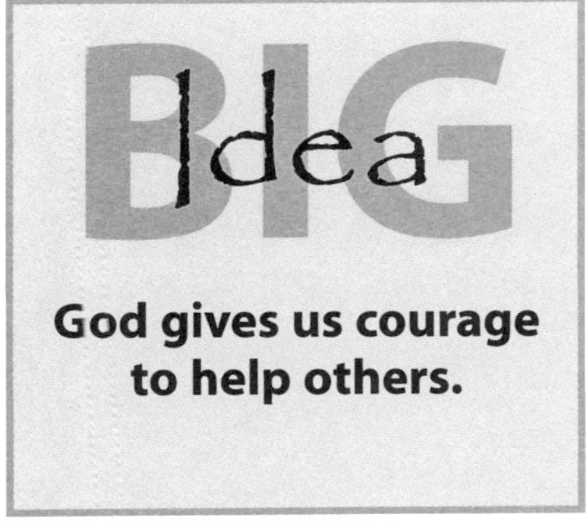

God gives us courage to help others.

LR = Learner Resource
TCK = Teacher Class Kit
M&P = Materials and Preparation

Teacher Prayer

Faithful God, you have given us people through the ages who guide us, both by word and example. As I live each day, remind me that my words and actions may be all that other people will see of your love! Amen

Question for Reflection

Do you remember specific times when you sensed God's plan for your life? Have those times made your choices easier or more difficult?

Learner Goals

KNOW
the story of baby Moses and God's plan for him

GROW
to understand that ordinary people show courage and responsibility

SHOW
courage in discovering ways to help others

FACTOID

Levites were one of the tribes of Israel.

Bible Background

What Factors Shaped This Story?

A famine generations earlier in their own land had led the ancient Israelites to Egypt, where they prospered. Though the Israelites had lived in Egypt under favorable conditions, Pharaoh, a new ruler in Egypt, abandoned any hospitality toward the Israelites. Pharaoh feared the power of the Israelite people so he enslaved them. Despite—or perhaps because of—Pharaoh's oppression, the Israelite population continued to grow. Out of fear, Pharaoh ordered that all newborn males among the Hebrew people be killed at birth. Hiding her son was the Levite woman's act of resistance against Pharaoh's edict. The child she saved became the leader of the Israelite liberation.

What Is This Story About?

Though Pharaoh ordered male children killed because he recognized males as a threat to him, in this story it is women who resist Pharaoh's oppressive system. The child's mother saves his life by hiding him. She and the child's sister risk his life, hoping to save it by setting him adrift in a basket on the river. Pharaoh's daughter, having her maid rescue the infant from the river, recognized the child as Israelite or Hebrew, took pity on him, and raised him as her own. Through the intervention of the infant's sister, his own mother served as his wet nurse. It may be because of women's relatively higher status among the ancient Egyptians that Pharaoh's daughter could act so decisively and independently.

Why Is This Story Important?

God's will is accomplished in the events of day-to-day life. The ordinary is vehicle for the extraordinary. Women, who were not seen to have power, made choices and acted effectively in opposition to the most powerful person around. A Hebrew child who was saved became the liberator of his people. Something important came about through a sequence of simple human events. God's will that people be free is fulfilled in the simple acts of people like you and me.

Age-Level Connection

Children of all ages love the story of baby Moses in a basket on the river! Miriam's love for her brother guided her in helping him. Your learners will likely know how it feels to want to make a bad situation better. They can understand that God had a plan for Moses, and God chose Miriam to put the plan into action.

Ready for the Story (15 minutes)

Welcome the Witnesses

M&P *Display Poster E (Teacher Class Kit). Have Track 4, "Mo Mo Mo Moses" of the Witness CD (TCK) playing as the learners arrive.*
Greet the learners as they arrive. Review the Sessions 1-3 Big Ideas on Poster E. Point out today's Big Idea *(God gives us courage to help others)*. Tell about a time when, as a child, you felt called to do something courageous. It need not be a heroic act, but a time when you made a choice to help someone in an unusual way.

Story Warm-Up

M&P *Display Posters D and P (TCK). Locate Activity Card A (TCK) and Faith Trait stickers (Learner Resource). Have available the learners' copies of the Little Book of Faith Traits (see Session 1 "Story Warm-Up").*
Refer to Poster D, reviewing the Faith Traits you have learned so far *(generosity, obedience, and patience)*. Ask the learners if they had any opportunities to demonstrate patience this past week. What happened? Was it hard or easy to do? Then point to today's Faith Trait on the poster (*responsibility*). **Today's Faith Trait is *responsibility*. There are many times in life when we need courage in order to take responsibility for someone or something in our lives.** Ask a volunteer to distribute the Little Book of Faith Traits and Faith Trait stickers. Have the learners place today's sticker on its corresponding page. Then have a learner place today's marker from Activity Card A on Poster P. Collect and save the booklets for next time.

Story Fire-Up

M&P *Bring along a baby photograph of yourself. Have learners display the baby photographs they brought (see Session 3 "Wrapping It Up") at the center of your meeting area.*
Look at the photographs everyone brought today. For fun, mix all the photos together and then see if the group can guess who each baby is! Talk with the learners about when they were babies or toddlers. They likely won't remember being so young, but they may have heard stories from caregivers about that time from their lives. **How is life different for a baby than it is for an older child?** *(A baby sleeps in a crib, drinks milk from a bottle, plays with rattles, cries a lot.)* Take time to focus on the fact that caregivers work hard to keep babies safe and secure.

reeds, famine, hospitality, prosper

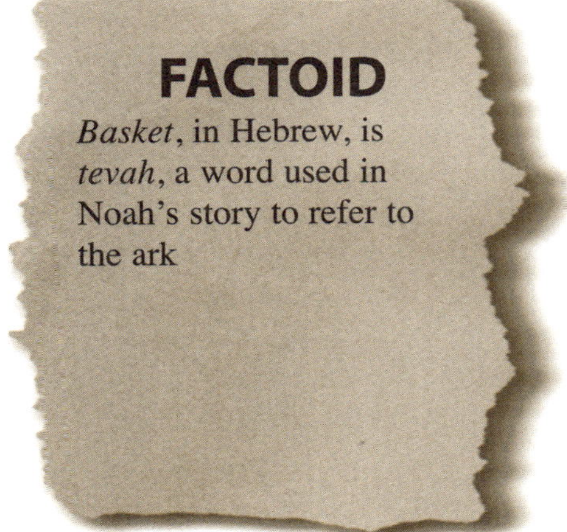

Transition Tip

Help learners develop their sense of responsibility by asking them to distribute materials, record attendance, read aloud, and offer prayers. Your positive comments and reinforcement will make them willing helpers.

Find "Thinking About Courage" on page 3 of the leaflet. Take turns reading the section aloud. Ask the learners to answer the questions. Have them share their answers with a partner.

Get things moving with a weaving game! Gather in a circle. Toss a ball of yarn to a learner, keeping hold of the loose end of the yarn strand. Continue in this way, having the learners toss the ball while holding onto the strand, connecting the whole group with a woven web!

Explore the Story (20 minutes)

Story Set-Up

M&P *Display Poster B (TCK). Place blue carpeting, rug, or blanket near the poster. Locate a woven basket suitable for a baby or doll.*

Have the learners gather on the blue rug or blanket, placing the basket at the center of the group. Point to Poster B and note some of the illustrations of Bible times children, calling attention to toys and household items pictured there. **When you were a baby, you may have slept in a bassinette or baby basket. In today's Bible story, baby Moses was placed inside a basket made of reeds that grew along the river. The reeds were cut, woven together, and sealed with a special kind of pitch that made the basket waterproof. Who can tell me why baby Moses was placed inside such a basket?** *(Allow time for the learners to share their thoughts.)*

Storytelling

M&P *Distribute Leaflet 4 (LR) and crayons or markers. Have Bibles available.*

Have the learners find "Hidden Picture" on page 1 of the leaflet. Distribute crayons or markers and give them time to complete the activity, revealing baby Moses among the reeds. Next, ask learners to look at "A Little History" on page 1. Ask volunteers to read aloud the picture caption that tells about what happened before today's Bible story. Distribute Bibles and help the learners locate Exodus 2:1-10. Remind them that Exodus is the second book in the Old Testament. Take turns reading the Bible text aloud. Then turn to page 2 of the leaflet. Read through the "Words to Know" and then work together to complete the Bible story questions.

Story Follow-Up

M&P *Have Leaflet 4 (LR) available.*

Ask learners to share their thoughts about the "Think About It" question on page 2 of the leaflet. **How do you think Moses' mother felt when she placed him in the basket?** *(Sad, afraid, uncertain she was doing the right thing.)* **How might she have felt when the princess asked her to care for Moses?** *(Thankful to God, happy, relieved.)* Remind them that God calls all of us to be courageous at some time in our lives. When we trust God, we can find the courage to help others even when it's hard to do.

Live the Story (25 minutes)

Ways to Witness

M&P *Have slips of paper and pencils available. Place the basket used earlier in the session at the center of the group.*

Ask the learners to think of ways they can show courage in the coming week. Offer examples, such as praying for someone who is difficult to love, apologizing to someone for a disagreement, offering forgiveness to someone who has wronged them in some way, being a friend to a less popular classmate at school, and so forth. Ask each learner to write his or her courageous idea on a slip of paper. When everyone is ready, have learners take turns tossing their papers into the basket, sharing their ideas if they wish. After everyone has participated, offer a prayer asking God for courage to help others.

Kids Create

M&P *For Woven Windsock: Have sheets of construction paper (one per learner), 1" (2.5 cm) wide strips of construction paper in a variety of colors, scissors, stapler, and glue. For Puzzle Piece Picture Frame: Have small picture frame matte boards (available at craft stores) or thin cardboard cut into small picture frames, an assortment of old puzzle pieces, glue, fast drying acrylic paint in a variety of colors, paint brushes, and water for clean-up. Make a sample of the project you choose.*

Woven Windsock: Show learners a completed windsock. Demonstrate how to fold a sheet of construction paper in half, cutting slits through the fold at 1" (2.5 cm) intervals, without cutting all the way to the end of the paper. Open the paper and weave several strips of colorful construction paper through the slits, leaving gaps between them. Trim as needed and then roll the woven paper lengthwise, creating a tube shape. Staple the edges together. Push from both ends to make the center fold more pronounced. Glue a paper handle to the top.

Puzzle Piece Picture Frame: Show learners a completed frame. Give each learner a matte or cardboard picture frame. Have them glue puzzle pieces to the frame, layering them as they wish. If time allows, learners could paint the puzzle pieces before gluing them to the frame. Suggest the learners ask a caregiver to help them attach a baby photograph to the back of the completed frame, displaying it in their home as a reminder that God helps us grow in courageous ways throughout our lives.

Wrapping It Up

M&P *Display Poster C (TCK). Have Leaflet 4 (LR) available.*

Point to Egypt on Poster C and remind the learners that Pharaoh made life very difficult for the Israelites. Emphasize how courageous Moses' mother and sister were to save him from this cruel ruler. Talk about the Witness Words that appear on page 4 of the leaflet. Help learners define the words and tell how they relate to today's Bible story. Remind them to share the activities on page 4 with their families. Have everyone collect their leaflets, Bibles, baby photographs, and completed projects to take home. Then pray: **Dear Lord, just as the people in today's story had courage, give us courage every day! Amen**

Teacher Boost

Sometimes it takes courage to just make it through the day. Many people say that helping others helps them get through lonely or sad times. Try it and see!

Witnesses in the World

Contact a local foster care agency and ask if birthday gifts are needed for the children served by the program. Have your class sponsor a church-wide collection of toys and clothing that could be given to foster care children.

Play Track 4 of the Witness CD (TCK). Whisper "God gives us courage to help others" to each learner as he or she leaves.

Moses Trusts God

Bible Text

Exodus 14:1-30

Key Verse

But Moses said to the people, "Do not be afraid, stand firm, and see the deliverance that the LORD will accomplish for you today."
Exodus 14:13

LR = Learner Resource
TCK = Teacher Class Kit
M&P = Materials and Preparation

Session at a Glance	What You Need	What Learners Do
Ready for the Story (15 minutes)		
Welcome the Witnesses	• Poster E and Witness CD (TCK), CD player, sticky notepaper	• Review Big Ideas and learn the Big Idea for Session 5.
Story Warm-Up	• Posters D and P (TCK), Activity Card A (TCK), Faith Trait stickers (LR), learners' copies of the Little Book of Faith Traits	• Review Faith Traits from Sessions 1-4, and learn today's Faith Trait: *boldness*.
Story Fire-Up	• Nothing	• Talk about trips they have taken and play a game.
Explore the Story (20 minutes)		
Story Set-Up	• Poster C (TCK), Leaflet 5 (LR), backpack or suitcase, travel items	• Complete a maze and read a diary entry.
Storytelling	• Witness CD (TCK), Leaflet 5 and Session 5 stickers (LR), CD player	• Listen to a recording of today's Bible story and read a newspaper account of the story.
Story Follow-Up	• Leaflet 5 (LR), chalkboard/chalk or chart paper/marker, Bible time props and costumes	• Write an account of the Israelites' journey.
Live the Story (25 minutes)		
Ways to Witness	• Chart paper, markers, crayons, colored pencils	• Make a map of the community and talk about witnessing to God's love.
Kids Create	• Shoe boxes or other small boxes, scissors, glue, markers, paper scraps, other craft items • Clear cellulose acetate paper, transparent tape, permanent fine-tipped markers, a clear votive candle holder	• Make a Bible Story Diorama or a "God Guides Me" Candle Slipcover.
Wrapping It Up	• Leaflet 5 (LR)	• Review the Bible story and Witness Words. Pray together.

Bible Background

What Factors Shaped This Story?

God called Moses to lead the Israelite people out of slavery. A series of confrontations in which Moses showed the power of God against Pharaoh culminated in a plague of death upon the firstborn sons of Egyptian families. At this, Pharaoh begged Moses and the Israelites to leave. They went out of Egypt and out of slavery. God led them safely into the wilderness toward the Red Sea.

What Is This Story About?

Even the plague of death does not temper Pharaoh's arrogance. He still does not take seriously God's power and sovereignty, so God sets a trap for him. Pharaoh knows the Israelites' weakness and vulnerability wandering in the wilderness and, disregarding the power of God, sends all his military might against a ragtag band of newly freed slaves.

Nor are the Israelites clear about what's going on. Seeing the Egyptians in hot pursuit, already forgetting what God has done, the Israelites blame Moses for the recapture they anticipate. Even Moses doesn't understand. He says that the Lord will fight for them. To which God says, "Why do you cry out to me?" (verse 15). God was with Moses through repeated confrontations with Pharaoh. God is with Moses and the Israelites now. All they need to do is move forward, relying on God's power. God will work with them, in them, and through them.

Moses does as the Lord commands. The waters of the sea part and the Israelites go across on dry land. In the same way, when the Israelites are safely across with the Egyptians in pursuit, the waters return and drown Pharaoh's military—vehicles, army, weapons, and all.

Why Is This Story Important?

The powerful can be arrogant. God stands with the oppressed and wills freedom. Did the waters actually part? Whether they did or not, God's power delivered the Israelites safely from the hands of their oppressor to freedom and a new life. Beside God, the power of this world comes to naught.

Age-Level Connection

Moving away from home, school, and friends can be traumatic for children at any age. Going on a long trip may produce different feelings. Third and fourth graders are able to express their feelings about either experience. Help them make a connection between their experiences and those of the Israelite people in today's story.

Teacher Prayer

Sometimes, God, it is hard to trust. Help me to grow in faith, boldly remaining obedient to you. Amen

Question for Reflection

God led the Israelites with a pillar of fire and a cloud. How has God led you?

Learner Goals

KNOW
the story about Moses and the Israelites traveling through the wilderness

GROW
in the knowledge of God's guidance in their lives

SHOW
others their love for God through their words and actions

FACTOID

The Israelites' route is uncertain. We know God did not lead them on the most direct route along the coast to their destination but took them a roundabout way (Exodus 13:17-18).

Ready for the Story (15 minutes)

Witness WORDS

plague, slavery, trust

Welcome the Witnesses

M&P *Display Poster E (Teacher Class Kit). Use sticky note paper to temporarily cover the words* world, promises, hope, *and* help *in the Sessions 1-4 Big Ideas listed on Poster E. Have songs from the Witness CD (TCK) playing as learners arrive.*

Warmly welcome learners to another session of Sunday school! Review Sessions 1-4 Big Ideas on Poster E by asking learners to recall the hidden words, offering hints as needed. Uncover the words as they recall them. Then read together today's Big Idea *(We can trust God when we are scared).*

Story Warm-Up

M&P *Display Posters D and P (TCK). Locate Activity Card A (TCK) and Faith Trait stickers (LR). Have available the learners' copies of the Little Book of Faith Traits (see Session 1 "Story Warm-Up").*

Point to today's Faith Trait (*boldness*) on Poster D. **What does it mean to be bold?** *(To face problems; not give into fears.)* **When we trust God to care for us, we can face each day with boldness.** Ask a volunteer to distribute copies of the Little Book of Faith Traits and Faith Trait stickers. Have learners place today's Faith Trait sticker on its corresponding page. Then ask a learner to place today's marker from Activity Card A on Poster P. Collect and save the booklets for next time.

FACTOID

Chariots and trained charioteers required technology and wealth. Slavery was one of the costs of maintaining Pharaoh's army.

Story Fire-Up

M&P *Nothing.*

Talk with the learners about trips they have taken. Where did they go? What did they do to get ready? What did they bring along? Play a game of "I'm going on vacation and I'm packing some...." The first player says the phrase, adding a word that begins with the same letter as his or her first name. For example, Jaedon might say, "I'm going on vacation and I'm packing some jelly beans." The next player repeats the phrase and "jelly beans," then adds another item that begins with the same letter as his or her first name. Continue in this way, with each learner adding a new item to the list. Save your turn until last and see if you can repeat all the items before adding your own! Then make a connection between the game and plans we make for our lives. **When we include God in our plans, our trip through life will be better!**

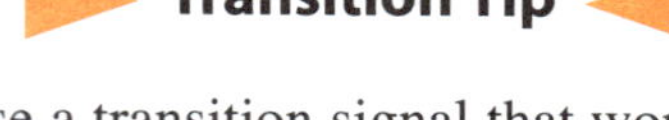

Transition Tip

Use a transition signal that works for you and your class. When it is time to change activities or listen to the teacher, flick the lights, ring a bell, or blow on a "train whistle."

Explore the Story (20 minutes)

Story Set-Up

M&P *Display Poster C (TCK). Have Leaflet 5 (LR) and pencils available. Bring along a backpack or suitcase that is packed with a few travel items, such as a toothbrush, snack, Bible, tickets, and a map.*

Place your backpack or suitcase at the center of your gathering space and say: **Earlier we talked about things we might pack for a trip. See if you can guess what I've packed today.** Describe each item within the suitcase and let the learners guess what it might be before showing it to them. Save the map for last. Then unfold the map and invite the learners to tell you what they know about it. What do the symbols and various colors signify? How does one determine the distance between places? **When we travel, a map helps us know where we are going.** Direct the learners' attention to Poster C. Point out the Israelites' journey as indicated on the map. Then distribute Leaflet 5 and pencils, inviting the learners to find their way through the maze on page 1. Ask a volunteer to read aloud "Dear Diary." **How is Hannah feeling about her family's journey?** *(Scared, excited.)* Ask learners to tell about similar feelings they have had when on a trip. Encourage them to tell about diaries or scrapbooks they have kept. Remind them that we can trust God when we are scared.

Storytelling

Have Witness CD (TCK), Leaflet 5 and Session 5 stickers (LR), and CD player available.

Now have the learners turn to page 2 of the leaflet. Read through the Bible Text, Big Idea and Key Verse together. Listen to "EXIT 14 News: Red Sea Rising" (Track 5) on the Witness CD. Distribute the newspaper headline stickers and have the learners place them on the leaflet's newspaper account of the Israelites' trip. Give the learners time to read and enjoy the newspaper account with a partner.

Story Follow-Up

M&P *Have available Leaflet 5 (LR), pencils, chalkboard and chalk or chart paper and marker. Provide a few simple Bible times props and costumes, such as a walking stick, shawl, and cloth belt.*

Ask the learners to find "You Were There!" on page 3 of their leaflets. What might it have been like to travel with Moses and the Israelites through the desert? Brainstorm with the learners, writing their thoughts and ideas on the chalkboard or chart paper. Then give them time to write a paragraph on page 3, describing their own account of the journey from the perspective of one of the people listed, or from someone else they choose. Then have volunteers dress in costume and read their accounts to the class.

We may not have a pillar of fire to guide us today, but God still shows us the way. Talk about such ways, including the Bible, Christian friends, and music.

Set chairs in two rows to represent the parted waters of the Red Sea. Then play a game of musical chairs as the learners ("Israelites") cross the sea to music on the Witness CD (TCK) or other contemporary Christian music of your choice.

Teacher Boost

We may not have a pillar of fire or cloud to guide us through each day, but we do have God's word. Make a point to read from your Bible each day!

Witnesses in the World

Moving to a new country can be a scary experience, especially for refugee families. Gather information about refugees living in your area. Find their country of origin on a map or globe. Talk about ways you could help lessen their fears.

GREAT good byes

Play lively music and invite learners to "travel" out the door in a creative way! Remind them that God is with them wherever they go!

Live the Story (25 minutes)

Ways to Witness

M&P *Have chart paper, markers, crayons, and colored pencils available. Write "Ways We Witness in* (name of your city or community)" *along the top of the chart paper.*

What are some ways we tell or show others we are people of faith? *(Inviting friends to church, helping those in need, accepting others.)* Encourage the learners to share their thoughts. Share your own ideas with the class. Then gather the group around the chart paper and invite them to create a map of your city or community. (If your group is large, form small groups to create maps.) Suggest that they include their homes, schools, church, and other places of interest on the map. Talk about ways the learners can witness at each location. Have them write their ideas next to each landmark. When the map is complete, display it in your class area as a reminder that we can trust God to help us witness boldly wherever we are.

Kids Create

M&P *For Bible Story Diorama: Locate a small box for each learner. Precut light and peep holes. Provide scissors, glue, markers, paper scraps, and other craft items. For Candle Slipcover: Cut clear cellulose acetate paper (available at craft stores) into 3" x 6" (8 cm x 15 cm) pieces. Have transparent tape and permanent fine-tipped markers available. Bring a clear votive candleholder. Make a sample of the project you choose.*

Bible Story Diorama: Show the learners a sample diorama. Talk about scenes from the Bible story the learners may like to create. Show them how to cut tabs at the bottom of their paper shapes so they will stand upright when glued inside the box (see diagram).

"God Guides Me" Candle Slipcover: Show learners a sample slipcover, taping it to a votive candleholder. Talk about the pillar of fire that guided the Israelites in today's story. **What symbols and words remind us that God guides us today?** *(A cross, shell, dove, "Jesus," "witness.")* Distribute cellulose acetate paper and markers. Have the learners create their own colorful designs on the paper, outlining them with black marker for a stained glass look. Have them ask a caregiver to help them tape the design around a votive candleholder. Suggest they use the candleholder during a family meal or devotional time.

Wrapping It Up

M&P *Have Leaflet 5 (LR) available.*

Remind the learners to collect their leaflets, Bibles, and completed projects to take home. Talk about the Witness Words that appear on page 4 of the learner leaflet. Help learners define the words and tell how they relate to today's Bible story. Point out the activities on page 4 and encourage everyone to share them with their families. Gather in a circle for prayer. Invite volunteers to name fears they have. After each fear is named say, as a group, "Teach us to trust you, God." When everyone has had an opportunity to participate, end the prayer with "Amen."

God Gives Us All We Need

Session at a Glance	What You Need	What Learners Do
Ready for the Story (15 minutes)		
Welcome the Witnesses	• Poster E and Witness CD (TCK), CD player	• Review Big Ideas and learn Big Idea for Session 6.
Story Warm-Up	• Posters D and P (TCK), Activity Card A (TCK), Faith Trait stickers (LR), the learners' copies of the Little Book of Faith Traits	• Review Faith Traits from Sessions 1-5, and learn the Faith Trait for today: *thankfulness*.
Story Fire-Up	• Envelopes, slips of numbered and blank paper, candy	• Learn about fairness.
Explore the Story (20 minutes)		
Story Set-Up	• Poster C (TCK), Leaflet 6 (LR)	• Review the journey of the Israelites and complete a word find puzzle.
Storytelling	• Reproducible Sheets C and D (TCK), Leaflet 6 and Session 6 stickers (LR), Bible	• Read a newspaper account of the Bible story and retell the story using puppets.
Story Follow-Up	• Leaflet 6 (LR), Bibles, crayons or markers	• Read Psalm 138:1-3 and draw or write about things they are thankful for.
Live the Story (25 minutes)		
Ways to Witness	• Nothing	• Create thanksgiving pantomimes.
Kids Create	• Enlarged photocopies of sample prayer, craft sticks, buttons, sequins, small shells, glue, magnet strips • Bread basket, non-toxic clay or dough, rolling pin, kitchen or craft tools, circular cookie cutter, baking sheets	• Make a Prayer Plaque or Bread Stone.
Wrapping It Up	• Leaflet 6 (LR)	• Review the Bible story and Witness Word. Offer prayers of thanksgiving.

Bible Text

Exodus 16:1-18

Key Verse

So Moses and Aaron said to all the Israelites, "In the evening you shall know that it was the LORD who brought you out of the land of Egypt, and in the morning you shall see the glory of the LORD." Exodus 16:6-7

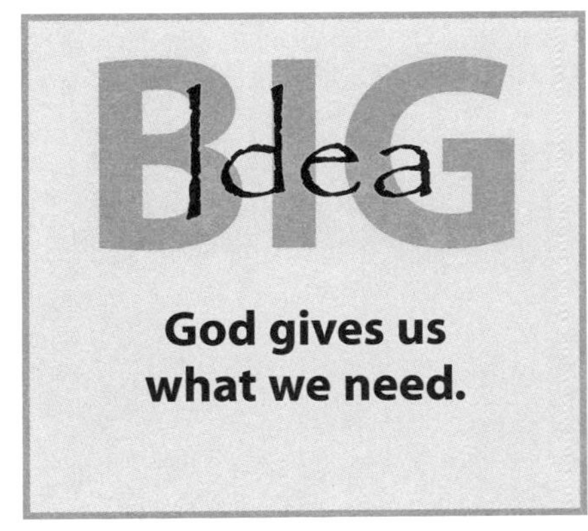

LR = Learner Resource
TCK = Teacher Class Kit
M&P = Materials and Preparation

Teacher Prayer

Generous God, thank you for giving me this opportunity to teach your children. May my words and thoughts reflect your wisdom and love today. Amen

Question for Reflection

How often do you remember to thank God for giving you everything you need?

Learner Goals

KNOW
that God provided food for the Israelites

GROW
in trusting that God always provides what we need

SHOW
awareness of the differences between needs and wants

FACTOID

Moses' brother, Aaron, was with Moses before Pharaoh and in the wilderness. Their sister, Miriam, gifted in music and dance, helped save Moses as an infant.

Bible Background

What Factors Shaped This Story?

Safely out of the hands of their Egyptian captors, the Israelites wander in the wilderness. Recently escaped from slavery and Pharaoh's exploitation, the Israelites have not yet learned a new life of freedom. Accustomed to the ways of imperial Egypt, they do not know how to survive in any other context, much less in the wilderness. Despite God's power that the Israelites witnessed in Egypt and despite God's delivering them safely from Pharaoh's army, the people still cannot imagine themselves as free and under God's care. They complain against Moses because of the hardships of being in the wilderness and they remember Egypt with longing.

What Is This Story About?

Which is more important: food or freedom? The Israelites complain to Moses that they'd be better off in slavery eating bread while the Egyptians eat meat than being free in the wilderness and hungry. The quail and manna God provides for them to eat shows that food and freedom are not traded off against one another. The Israelites gathered manna in the mornings. Some gathered more, some less (verse 17), perhaps because of differing ability based on size, strength, or stamina. When they measured the manna, each had what was needed. Contrary to the distribution of food under Egyptian slavery, God's food in the wilderness provided bread and meat for all according to their need, not too much or too little.

Why Is This Story Important?

When God calls us out of enslavement to new lives of freedom, God does not abandon us to learn new ways on our own. New living takes new learning. New choices teach new discernment. Freedom takes practice. A new way of life is made up of many, many new ways of thinking, doing, and being. Reliance on God's provision along the path that God calls us is how we manage to make our way to a new way of life.

Age-Level Connection

Third and fourth graders are at the center of the "marketplace" that advertisers often target. With constantly advancing technologies and media sources, our society is bombarded with messages telling us what we should want to have! Consequently, it isn't always easy for children to differentiate between needs and wants, but activities and discussions provided in this session can help.

Ready for the Story (15 minutes)

Welcome the Witnesses

M&P *Display Poster E (Teacher Class Kit). Have Track 6, "Wand'rin' Far And Wide," of the Witness CD (TCK) playing as learners arrive.*

Greet the learners as they arrive and invite them to listen to the CD song. Tell them they will continue to learn about the Israelites' journey through the wilderness today. Ask volunteers to help you read and review the Big Ideas from Sessions 1-5 that appear on Poster E. Then read together the Big Idea for today *(God gives us what we need).*

Story Warm-Up

M&P *Display Posters D and P (TCK). Locate Activity Card A (TCK) and Faith Trait stickers (LR). Have available the learners' copies of the Little Book of Faith Traits (see Session 1 "Story Warm-Up").*

Ask a volunteer to locate today's Faith Trait on Poster D (*thankfulness*). **When was the last time you said "thank you" to someone?** *(This morning when my mom made my breakfast, just now when Connor offered me a chair.)* Talk about how important it is to live thankful lives. When we do, we are witnessing to our faith! Have a learner distribute the Little Book of Faith Traits and Faith Trait stickers. Review the booklet pages for Sessions 1-5. Have learners place today's sticker on its corresponding page. Then have a learner place today's marker from Activity Card A on Poster P. Collect and save the booklets.

Story Fire-Up

M&P *Provide an envelope for each learner. Inside half of the envelopes, seal a slip of paper with a number (1-5) written on it. Seal the remaining envelopes with blank slips of paper. Have candy pieces available. Before serving any candy, always check with caregivers for learners who have food allergies. Provide an alternative, if necessary.*

Distribute the envelopes, telling the learners not to open them. Avoid giving envelopes with blank slips to those learners who may feel especially hurt to receive one. Tell the group that envelopes containing numbered slips may be exchanged for candies. Blank slips receive no candies. Invite the learners to trade envelopes if they wish, then open them. Distribute candies. **How did it feel to receive no candy?** *(Unfair.)* **Even though the candy isn't something you need, is it something you want?** *(Accept all answers.)* Now ask learners to think about our world. **What things do some people have plenty of, but other people have little or nothing of?** *(Food, money, possessions.)* **How does that make you feel?** *(Answers will vary.)* Thank the learners for their thoughtful discussion. Make sure to give candy to the learners who did not receive any.

Witness WORDS

survive, manna, thankfulness

FACTOID

Moses was basically a meek man and found it difficult to deal with the people's opposition, despite the miracles God performed through him.

Transition Tip

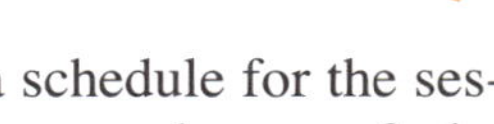

Displaying a schedule for the session can help some learners feel less anxious about what to expect and may help them focus on the activities.

Create columns on chart paper headed "Wants" and "Needs." Have learners glue on magazine pictures, indicating what they think are wants and needs. Does everyone agree? Do wants/needs differ in families? In countries?

More Movement

Help the learners create a jump rope prayer! Use this format or another of your choosing and let the learners jump rope to the rhythm: "Thank you, God, for ________ and ________. For ________ and ________, we give you thanks!"

Explore the Story (20 minutes)

Story Set-Up

M&P *Display Poster C (TCK). Have ready Leaflet 6 (LR) and pencils.* Ask a volunteer to point out the journey of Moses and the Israelites on Poster C as you review their story so far *(God chose Moses to lead the Israelites out of Egypt; God helped them escape Pharaoh's army at the Red Sea; in today's story they continue their long journey through the wilderness).* Ask the learners to tell about new experiences they have had while traveling, including new foods they have eaten along the way. **It can be fun to try new foods when we are traveling, but sometimes we miss the foods we enjoy at home. In today's Bible story, the Israelites miss the foods they enjoyed while living in Egypt.** Ask a volunteer to distribute the leaflets and pencils. Give the learners time to complete the "Missing Foods Puzzle" on page 1.

Storytelling

M&P *Make copies of Reproducible Sheets C and D (TCK) for each learner. Have available Leaflet 6 (LR). Locate the Session 6 sticker (LR). Have a Bible available.*

Now have the learners turn to page 2 in their leaflets. Ask volunteers to read the Bible Text, Big Idea, and Key Verse printed there. Read "Read All About It!" Distribute the stickers and have the learners add them to their leaflets as you read today's story to them from a Bible (Exodus 16:1-18). Then take time to read and discuss the newspaper account of the story that appears in the leaflet. Distribute the reproducible sheets and let the learners color and put together their puppets, then use them in small groups to retell the story.

Story Follow-Up

M&P *Have available Leaflet 6 (LR), Bibles, pencils, crayons or markers.* Remind the learners that God calls us to live thankful lives. When we do, we are witnessing to our faith. Turn to page 3 in the leaflet and have partners work together on the "Psalm of Thanksgiving" activity. When they finish this section, pray the psalm together. Then ask the learners to work independently on "What Are You Thankful For?" on page 3. Give them time to draw and write in the space provided. Tell them you will invite them to share some of the things they are thankful for during your closing prayer.

Live the Story (25 minutes)

Ways to Witness

M&P *Nothing.*

How do we show thanksgiving in our lives? Form three groups. Assign each group one of the following areas: *home, school,* and *world*. Have each group discuss ways we show thanks in its assigned area. Then have them create a pantomime that depicts one or more of their ideas. Invite each group to present its "thanksgiving pantomime" to the other groups, inviting the observers to guess what each group is portraying.

Kids Create

M&P *For Prayer Plaque: Enlarge and photocopy the sample prayer shown here on heavy copier paper for each learner. Cut each prayer to fit within a frame of four craft sticks. Have glue, magnetic strips, craft sticks, buttons, sequins, and small shells or other decorative craft items available. For Bread Stone: Bring a bread basket, purchased or homemade non-toxic clay that can be baked and reheated according to package/recipe directions, rolling pins, kitchen or craft items for making imprints in soft clay (straws, forks, rubber stamps), circular cookie cutter, and baking sheets if you will be baking the Bread Stones during the session. Otherwise, plan to bake the stones later and return them to the learners the next time you meet. Make a sample of the project you choose.*

Prayer Plaque: Show learners a sample Prayer Plaque. Give them copies of the prayer, and let them glue craft sticks around it, creating a frame. Then invite them to glue on decorative items. When the glue dries, attach a magnetic strip to the back of the plaque so that it can hang on a refrigerator.

Bread Stone: Place the Bread Stone you made inside a breadbasket. Explain to the group that, after an adult warms the stone in an oven and then places it inside a basket, warm bread or rolls can be placed on top of it. The stone will help keep the bread warm as it is served. Show the learners how to roll out the soft clay to a thickness of approximately 1" (2.5 cm), and then use a cookie cutter to cut a stone. Demonstrate how to imprint designs in the clay using the tools you provide. Bake the clay according to package/recipe directions, or tell learners you will return their finished stones to them the next time you meet.

Wrapping It Up

M&P *Have Leaflet 6 (LR) available.*

Have the learners collect their leaflets, Bibles and completed projects to take home. Look at the Witness Words on page 4 of the leaflet and ask them to tell how they relate to today's Bible story. Remind them to show their families the activities on page 4. Have them refer to "What Are You Thankful For?" on page 3 of their leaflets as you close with prayer: **Generous God, you always give us what we need, but sometimes we forget to thank you. Today we'd like to thank you for…** *(Invite learners to offer their prayers of thanks.)* **Thank you, God, for all you give us! Amen**

Teacher Boost

Each day this week, take time before each meal to truly thank God for always providing what you need!

Witnesses in the World

Is there an organization that serves homeless people in your community? Arrange for a guest speaker to visit during today's session, or make plans for your class to help serve a meal to people in need.

Go Global!

Read the Go Global! activity on Reproducible Sheets S and T (TCK). See page 3.

GREAT good byes

As the learners leave today, play Track 6 of the Witness CD. Remind them that God's love reaches us wherever we are!

God Is Always With Us

Bible Text

Joshua 6:1-20

Key Verse

Be strong and courageous; do not be frightened or dismayed, for the LORD your God is with you wherever you go. Joshua 1:9

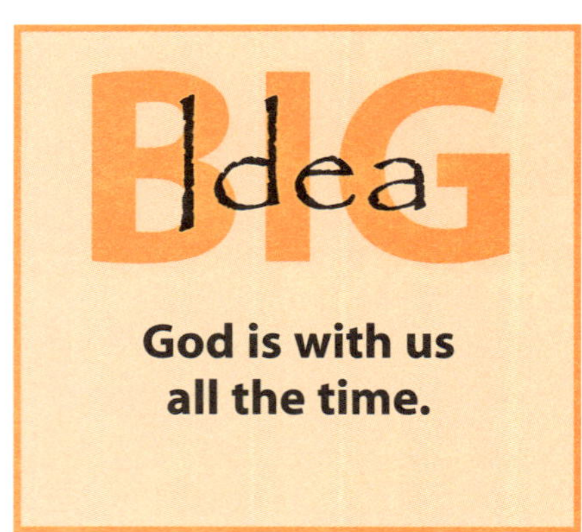

Session at a Glance	What You Need	What Learners Do
Ready for the Story (15 minutes)		
Welcome the Witnesses	• Poster E and Witness CD (TCK), CD player	• Review Big Ideas and discuss today's Big Idea.
Story Warm-Up	• Posters D and P (TCK), Activity Card A (TCK), Faith Trait stickers (LR), the learners' copies of the Little Book of Faith Traits, dictionary	• Review Faith Traits from Sessions 1-6, and learn the Faith Trait for today: *perseverance*.
Story Fire-Up	• Large blanket or rug, building blocks	• Build a block city.
Explore the Story (20 minutes)		
Story Set-Up	• Leaflet 7 (LR), pencils	• Read Bible verses and complete a dot-to-dot activity.
Storytelling	• Leaflet 7 (LR), Witness CD (TCK), CD player	• Discover the Key Verse in code and listen to the Bible story.
Story Follow-Up	• Leaflet 7 (LR), Activity Card B1 (TCK), Bibles, markers, reusable adhesive putty or thumbtacks	• Retell the Bible story by sequencing picture cards.
Live the Story (25 minutes)		
Ways to Witness	• Nothing	• Talk about promises.
Kids Create	• Construction paper, fine-tipped markers, adult scissors, newspaper • Yarn or cording, pony beads	• Make a 3-D Bible City or a Promises Bracelet.
Wrapping It Up	• Leaflet 7 (LR), CD of marching music, CD player	• Review the Bible story and Witness Words. Pray together.

LR = Learner Resource
TCK = Teacher Class Kit
M&P = Materials and Preparation

Bible Background

What Factors Shaped This Story?

The Israelites fled Egyptian slavery. God promised to deliver them into a land where they could live as free people. After two generations of wilderness wandering, they were free enough from the ways of slavery and ready for new life in a new land. Historians believe that other tribes, inspired by the story of flight from slavery and by the life of freedom promised by Israel's God, joined those who had fled Egypt. God called Joshua to lead the people into the promised land.

What Is This Story About?

In preparation for the conquest of Jericho, the Lord instructs Joshua what the people are to do. God has determined that the land will be theirs. By marching, blowing horns, and finally shouting, they will conquer the city. Following this seemingly silly plan constitutes people's obedience to God. Though the Israelites had armed men (6:9, 13), the priests are the primary actors, blowing horns and carrying the Ark of the Covenant, sign of God's presence. It is troubling to learn the story that God led one people in conquest of another. Historians speculate that the way of life established by the Israelites in the promised land was, at least at the outset, one of freedom and justice displacing the local systems of exploitation.

Why Is This Story Important?

Is the story literally true? Whatever the facts, the story tells that God kept the promises made to Moses and the people. In partnership with God, God's leaders chosen for the people continued to accomplish what seemed otherwise impossible.

Age-Level Connection

In this uncertain world that we live in, children often feel afraid or unsure of what the future will bring to their lives. As you explore God's promises in today's session, your learners will hear the comforting news that God's promises never change. God is with us all the time.

Teacher Prayer

Thank you, God, for showing your presence to me every day! Thank you for all things, small or large, that help me keep my focus on you. Amen

Question for Reflection

Which promise from God do you especially cling to? How has the assurance of that promise shaped your faith?

Learner Goals

KNOW
the story of Joshua at Jericho

GROW
in understanding that God is always with them

SHOW
security in their role as children of God

FACTOID

The story of Jericho begins the conquest of Canaan, which the Israelites occupied as the promised land.

Ready for the Story (15 minutes)

Witness WORDS

perseverance, courage

Welcome the Witnesses

M&P *Display Poster E (Teacher Class Kit). Play music from the Witness CD (TCK) as the learners arrive.*
Ask volunteers to read the Big Ideas for Sessions 1-6, using Poster E. Then read together today's Big Idea *(God is with us all the time)*. **Which Big Ideas contain promises so far?** *(Allow time for the learners to reflect and respond.)* **When do you especially think about God's promises?** *(Answers will vary.)* Share your own thoughts and tell learners they will learn more about God's promises today.

Story Warm-Up

M&P *Display Posters D and P (TCK). Locate Activity Card A (TCK) and Faith Trait stickers (Learner Resource). Have ready the learners' copies of the Little Book of Faith Traits (see Session 1 "Story Warm-Up"). Have a dictionary available.*
Point to Poster D and have the learners read the Faith Traits you have already explored (*generosity, obedience, patience, responsibility, boldness,* and *thankfulness*). Then read together today's Faith Trait: *perseverance*. **What does it mean to persevere at something?** If the learners are unsure of the word's meaning, work together to find it in a dictionary and read its definition. Then ask volunteers to define the Faith Trait in their own words. Next, ask a learner to distribute copies of the Little Book of Faith Traits and Faith Trait stickers. Have learners place today's sticker on its corresponding page. Then have a learner place today's marker from Activity Card A on Poster P. Collect and save the booklets for next time.

FACTOID

Of the adults who set out from Egypt, only two survived to enter the promised land of Canaan 40 years later. One of these was Joshua.

Story Fire-Up

M&P *Provide a large blanket or rug and a container of building blocks.*
Spread the blanket or rug on the floor and dump the blocks in the center of it. Encourage the learners to work together to build a Bible time city. Talk about how an ancient city would be different from a modern city. *(Skyscrapers were not part of ancient cities; there would probably have been a central area with a well where people would gather for water and trading; a wall may have built around the city for protection.)* As the learners work together, tell them that today's Bible story takes place at a city named Jericho. God sent the Israelites there to capture the city in a most unusual way.

Transition Tip

Have the learners stand in a single file line, march around the room three times, then sit down again before continuing with the session.

Explore the Story (20 minutes)

Story Set-Up

M&P *Have Leaflet 7 (LR) and pencils ready.*
Gather the learners together in a circle. Ask them to think about times when they have made a promise to someone, or someone has made a promise to them. **How do you feel when someone doesn't follow through on a promise?** *(Hurt, disappointed, it's hard to trust that person.)* Ask a volunteer to distribute the leaflets and invite everyone to find "God's Promises For Us" on page 1. Read through the introduction to the activity and then invite partners to complete it together. Tell learners that the Bible verses listed on this page can bring them comfort when they feel sad, lonely, or afraid. Encourage learners to choose one of the verses and memorize it at home today! Then give learners time to read "A City's Walls" on page 1 of the leaflet and complete the picture of Jericho by adding people, animals, and other Bible times items. How does this picture compare to the block city they built earlier?

If you know American Sign Language, try teaching the learners today's Key Verse using ASL. If not, help the group create hand or body motions to express the verse.

Storytelling

M&P *Have ready Leaflet 7 (LR) and Track 7 of the Witness CD (TCK). Locate a CD player and pencils.*
Now have the learners turn to page 3 in their leaflets. Find "Crack the Code!" and give everyone time to complete the activity, revealing today's Key Verse *(Be strong and courageous; do not be frightened or dismayed, for the Lord your God is with you wherever you go)*. Read the verse in unison after everyone has "cracked" it. Then ask the learners to locate "Joshua's Journal" on page 2. Ask a volunteer to pretend to be Joshua as he or she reads the section aloud. After the reading, play "Live Action Sports: Crumble at Jericho" on Track 7 of the Witness CD. **Today's Bible story is a reminder that, even during difficult times, God is with us.**

More Movement

Move outdoors and play Track 18 of the Witness CD (TCK) as learners reenact today's story while marching around your church building.

Story Follow-Up

M&P *Prepare Activity Card B1 (TCK). Have Leaflet 7 (LR), Bibles, markers, reusable adhesive putty, or thumbtacks available.*

Randomly distribute the activity cards to several learners and invite them to gather at the front of the classroom. Challenge them to stand in order so that the cards retell today's story. Invite other learners to offer help and read portions of the story from their Bibles as needed. After the learners are in correct order, have them display the cards on a wall or bulletin board. Then give everyone time to complete "You Are The Reporter!" on page 3 of the leaflet. Encourage learners to use their Bibles to answer the questions. Invite them to draw a picture that shows a scene from the story.

Live the Story (25 minutes)

Ways to Witness

 *Nothing.*

Sometimes we may promise to do something, but then something better to do comes along. For example, you promise to clean your pet rabbit's cage, but then your friend invites you over to play video games. Encourage the learners to share similar situations from their lives. How do they feel when they keep a promise? How do they feel when they break a promise? What can be the result of keeping or breaking promises? Form small groups and ask each one to role-play a situation in which someone must decide whether or not to keep a promise. After the role-plays ask: **When does it require courage to keep a promise? How does God help us persevere in keeping promises?**

Teacher Boost

Your faithfulness to God is evident to your class! The time you take to prepare each session and the way you listen to and care for each learner is noticed and appreciated!

Kids Create

M&P *For 3-D Bible City: Provide assorted colors of construction paper, pencils, fine-tipped markers, adult scissors, and newspapers. For Promises Bracelet: Have 12" (30 cm) strands of colorful yarn or cording (one per learner), scissors, and assorted colors of pony beads. Make a sample of the project you choose.*

3-D Bible City: Show learners a sample city. Have them choose a sheet of construction paper and then demonstrate how to draw shapes on the paper, including buildings, trees, and bushes, leaving space between each shape. Suggest they add details with fine-tipped markers. Next, have them place their city drawings on several layers of newspaper as they carefully push the point of a scissors through and cut around three sides of each shape, leaving the bottom edge uncut so the shape can be folded forward .

Promises Bracelet: Show the learners a completed bracelet. Distribute strands of yarn or cording. As the learners choose beads for their bracelets, talk about the significance various colors have in our Christian faith. For example, purple symbolizes royalty, white purity, and green reminds us of the promise of new life we have through Jesus. Encourage the learners to string beads on their bracelet using colors and patterns that remind them of God's promises. Whenever they wear their bracelets, they can remember that God is with them at all times!

Witnesses in the World

God needs people to lead the way! Talk with a pastor or another congregational leader about leadership roles for your class. Maybe you could welcome worshipers before a service, start a recycling program, or clean up around the church grounds.

Wrapping It Up

M&P *Have Leaflet 7 (LR) available. If possible, play a CD of marching music.*

Remind the learners to collect their leaflets, Bibles, and completed projects. Ask them to help you clean up the class area as they move to marching music. Then gather everyone together in a circle. Read the Witness Words on page 4 of the leaflet and ask volunteers to use each word in a sentence that relates to today's Bible story. Remind the learners to try the activities on page 4 with their families. Then ask a volunteer to begin a prayer. Ask another volunteer to be ready to end the prayer. Invite all other learners to add their own spoken prayers in between.

Play some lively praise or marching music as the learners leave today. Remind them that God is always with them wherever they go!

Called by God

Session at a Glance	What You Need	What Learners Do
Ready for the Story (15 minutes)		
Welcome the Witnesses	• Poster E and Witness CD (TCK), CD player	• Review Big Ideas and discuss the Big Idea for Session 8.
Story Warm-Up	• Posters D and P (TCK), Activity Card A (TCK), Faith Trait stickers (LR), the learners' copies of the Little Book of Faith Traits	• Review Faith Traits from Session 1-7, and learn today's Faith Trait *obedience*.
Story Fire-Up	• Poster G (TCK)	• Play a game of "I Spy."
Explore the Story (20 minutes)		
Story Set-Up	• Leaflet 8 (LR), Bibles	• Learn about Bible people who have been called by God.
Storytelling	• Witness CD (TCK), Leaflet 8 (LR), CD player, Bibles	• Unscramble the Key Verse and read the Bible story.
Story Follow-Up	• Leaflet 8 and Session 8 stickers (LR), markers or crayons	• Solve riddles to discover people who have been called by God.
Live the Story (25 minutes)		
Ways to Witness	• Drawing paper, markers, crayons	• Talk about inviting friends to Sunday school and worship.
Kids Create	• Copies of Reproducible Sheet G (TCK), liquid starch, disposable bowls, paintbrushes, tissue paper scraps, paper toweling • Index cards, fine-tipped markers, gel pens, self-sticking magnetic strips	• Make a Stained Glass Window or "God Calls Me" Magnet.
Wrapping It Up	• Poster K and Witness CD (TCK), Leaflet 8 (LR), small mirror	• Review the Bible story and Witness Words. Pray together.

Bible Text

Judges 6:1-24

Key Verse

The angel of the LORD appeared to him and said to him, "The LORD is with you." Judges 6:12

God wants us to worship and serve only God.

LR = Learner Resource
TCK = Teacher Class Kit
M&P = Materials and Preparation

Teacher Prayer

God, help me clear my mind so that I can hear your call. I pray today for all of my learners and their families, that you will bless them and be a part of their lives. Amen

Question for Reflection

Has God ever called you to do something you didn't really want to do? How did you respond?

Learner Goals

KNOW
the story of Gideon's call from God

GROW
in knowledge regarding the worship space of their church

SHOW
understanding of what it means to be called by God today

FACTOID

While the Midianites in this story are enemies of Israel, in Exodus (2:15b-22) Moses lives among the Midianites and marries the daughter of a Midianite priest.

Bible Background

What Factors Shaped This Story?

The book of Judges witnesses to local conflicts over the Israelite settlement of Canaan. Continuing contests over Israelite occupation are the result of the people's disobedience toward God. The establishment of a just and equitable society was not easy. There was conflict among the Israelites and other new settlers as well as with those already on the land. After Joshua's death, God raised up judges to lead the people. The judges included Othniel, Ehud, Deborah, Gideon, and Jephthah. Not until the establishment of kingship in Israel (1 Samuel 8) was there anything like a state or bureaucratic leadership.

What Is This Story About?

Forgetting their deliverance from slavery and the way of life with God that would keep them free, the Israelites turned away from God and became subject to the Midianites. The Israelites struggled to eke out a living. Like those we call guerrilla fighters, the Israelites hid in the "mountains, caves, and strongholds" (6:2). The Midianites routed Israelite settlements, destroying their crops and livestock and ravishing the land itself. When the Israelites cried to the Lord for help, a prophet of the Lord reminded the people of their deliverance from slavery and their unfaithfulness toward the Lord.

A messenger of the Lord went to Gideon, proclaiming that the Lord was with him. Gideon questioned God's presence with the people given all the terrible things that were taking place under the Midianites. Despite the people's disobedience and Gideon's believing that God had abandoned them, the Lord called Gideon to deliver the people.

Why Is This Story Important?

We easily forget God's continuing presence and power in our lives. When we turn away from God and then suffer hardship alone, we blame God for turning away from us. Gideon thinks that God has abandoned the people, when it is the people who have turned their backs on God. Still, despite the people's unfaithfulness and without their repentance, when they cried to God, God called a leader to deliver them.

Age-Level Connection

Third and fourth graders are developing a definite sense of right and wrong. Gideon's story will likely be of interest to them. They may share Gideon's concerns—that God had forgotten the people and let terrible things happen to them. However, they may also begin to understand that God had a plan for the people. When they trusted and obeyed God, their lives were blessed.

Ready for the Story (15 minutes)

Welcome the Witnesses

M&P *Display Poster E (Teacher Class Kit). Have songs from the Witness CD (TCK) playing as the learners arrive.*
Greet everyone and invite partners to read together the Sessions 1-7 Big Ideas from Poster E. Then read aloud today's Big Idea together *(God wants us to worship and serve only God)*. **This Big Idea sounds like one of the Ten Commandments. Does anyone know which one?** *(I am the Lord your God… you shall have no other gods before me (Exodus 20:2-3).)*

Story Warm-Up

M&P *Display Posters D and P (TCK). Locate Activity Card A (TCK) and Faith Trait stickers (Learner Resource). Have ready the learners' copies of the Little Book of Faith Traits (see Session 1 "Story Warm-Up").*
Refer to Poster D and review the Faith Traits from Sessions 1-7 (*generosity, obedience, patience, responsibility, boldness, thankfulness*, and *perseverance*). Then point to today's Faith Trait (*obedience*). Ask learners to share what they remember about that Faith Trait from the last time it was discussed (Session 2).

Next, ask a volunteer to distribute copies of the Little Book of Faith Traits and Faith Trait stickers. Have the learners place today's sticker on its corresponding page. Then ask a learner to place today's marker from Activity Card A on Poster P. Collect and save the booklets for next time.

Story Fire-Up

M&P *Display Poster G (TCK).*
Gather around Poster G and play a game of "I Spy" with the learners. Locate an area or object on the poster, such as a pulpit. **I spy a pulpit!** The first learner to correctly point to the pulpit begins the next round. If learners are unfamiliar with the correct names for various objects, have them describe the objects instead (for example, "I spy something that holds water" for a baptismal font). Play for a few minutes and then ask: **How are these illustrations similar to our worship space? How are they different?** *(Answers will vary.)* **There are many ways people worship God. Some people prefer worshiping in a sanctuary with an organ, choir, and hymns. Other people prefer a smaller worship space with contemporary Christian songs and guitar music. Regardless of how or where we worship, it's important to remember that God wants us to worship and serve only God!**

Witness WORDS

proclaim, worship

FACTOID

"The angel of the LORD" (Judges 6:11) may be understood to be a messenger of God or as God appearing. In either case, the message is God's own.

 **Transition Tip** 

Invite the learners to join you in a circle. Pass a small mirror around the circle. Tell the learners to look in the mirror to see someone who is called by God!

Explore the Story (20 minutes)

Story Set-Up

M&P *Have Leaflet 8 (LR), pencils, and Bibles available.*

If you tried the Transition Tip, ask: **Were you surprised when I asked you to look in the mirror to see someone who is called by God?** *(Some learners may think that only Bible people, pastors, or missionaries are called by God.)* **What does it mean to be called by God?** *(Help learners realize that God calls each of us to share the good news of God's love through our words and actions.)* Share an example from your life of how God has called you, such as teaching this Sunday school class! Or share an example from the life of someone you know. Encourage learners to share examples from their own lives as well. Then distribute the leaflets and work with the learners to locate the Bible references listed on page 1 under "Who Heard God's Call?" Let the learners complete this activity with a partner.

Storytelling

M&P *Have Track 8 of the Witness CD (TCK) ready to play. Have Leaflet 8 (LR), pencils, and Bibles available.*

Ask the learners to turn to page 3 in their leaflets. Read through the directions for the "Bible Verse Scramble," having the learners write the words correctly on the scroll. *(Answer: The angel of the Lord appeared to him and said to him, "The Lord is with you." Judges 6:12)* Then read aloud the Key Verse together.

Next, continue with the Bible story activity, "God Calls Gideon." Work together as a class to locate Judges 6:1-24 in your Bibles and then fill in the missing words on page 2 of the leaflet. When complete, take turns reading the story from the leaflet. **How did Gideon feel when God called him?** *(Not very happy; Gideon felt that God had abandoned him because of all the terrible things that had happened.)* **Despite what Gideon believed, God called him to carry out God's plan.** Then play Track 8, "Giddy-up Gideon," on the Witness CD and invite the learners to sing along!

Story Follow-Up

M&P *Have Leaflet 8 and Session 8 stickers (LR), pencils, and markers or crayons available.*

Have the learners find "They Answered God's Call" on page 3 in their leaflets. Take turns reading the riddles aloud. Distribute stickers and have learners match them with the riddles. *(Answers: Mother Teresa, Brother Andrew, Corrie Ten Boom, Billy Graham.)* Ask the learners to tell what they know about these people. Share any additional information you may have. **God not only calls church leaders and missionaries—God calls all of us to worship and serve God!** Continue with "How has God Called You?" Have learners write a riddle or draw a picture that describes how they worship and serve God.

Tour the worship space in your church. If possible, arrange for a pastor or altar guild member to join you, explaining the use of colors, paraments, vestments, and chancel furnishings.

Play a favorite song from the Witness CD (TCK) and encourage the learners to bend, stretch, or move in place before continuing with the session.

Live the Story (25 minutes)

Ways to Witness

M&P *Gather drawing paper, markers, and crayons.*
Talk with the learners about inviting friends to Sunday school or worship services. Have any of them invited a friend so far this year? Have they ever been invited to attend Sunday school or worship with a friend? **Sometimes the only reason people haven't come to Sunday school or worship services is because no one has ever invited them!** Encourage the learners to invite someone they know to come with them to Sunday school, a worship service, or a special church event sometime soon. If time permits, have the learners design special invitations to give to someone they know.

Kids Create

M&P *For Stained Glass Window: Make a copy of Reproducible Sheet G (TCK) for each learner. Bring liquid starch in small disposable bowls, paintbrushes, tissue paper scraps, and paper toweling for clean up. For "God Calls Me" Magnet: Provide index cards cut to 2" x 3½" (5 cm x 9 cm), fine tipped markers, gel pens, and self-sticking magnetic strips. Make a sample of the project you choose.*
Stained Glass Window: Show learners a completed project. Distribute copies of the reproducible sheet and demonstrate how to paint the window shapes with liquid starch. Next, lay various colors of tissue paper scraps over the wet starch. When the window design is complete, spread another layer of starch over the entire project. Allow to dry until next time, if necessary.
"God Calls Me" Magnet: Show learners the magnet you made. Have each learner design a "business card" that says, "God calls me!" The card should also include the learner's name, and something he or she believes God has called him or her to do *("God calls me to be kind;" "God calls me to sing in the children's choir")*. Encourage them to also add a decorative border and a favorite design that symbolizes their desire to worship and serve God, such as a cross, heart, rainbow, or musical note. Attach a magnetic strip to the back of the card and encourage learners to use them at home.

Wrapping It Up

M&P *Display Poster K (TCK) next to your classroom exit. Have Leaflet 8 (LR) and a small mirror available. Play music from the Witness CD or another CD of praise music as the learners clean up the class area.*
Remind the learners to collect their leaflets, Bibles, and completed projects. Talk about the Witness Words on page 4 of the leaflet. Ask learners to tell how the words relate to today's Bible story. Encourage the learners to try the activities on page 4 with their families. Then pray together: **God, we thank you for giving us ways to worship and serve you. Help us remember that we are called to share the good news of your never-ending love. Amen**

Before departing, read the heading on Poster K and then direct each learner to look into a small mirror. Remind the learners that God calls each of them!

Teacher Boost

The learners in your group come from a variety of family backgrounds and experiences. Your acceptance of them as children of God and your genuine interest in their lives are great witnesses to God's love and care.

Witnesses in the World

Keeping your church's worship space tidy is a big job, especially when people leave worship folders and other items in the pews. Perhaps your class could offer to serve one Sunday a month as a "clean-up crew" between or after services.

GREAT good byes

Whisper a special good news message to each learner as he or she leaves today.

Faithful Friends

Bible Text

Ruth 1

Key Verse

"Where you go, I will go; Where you lodge, I will lodge; your people shall by my people, and your God my God." Ruth 1:16

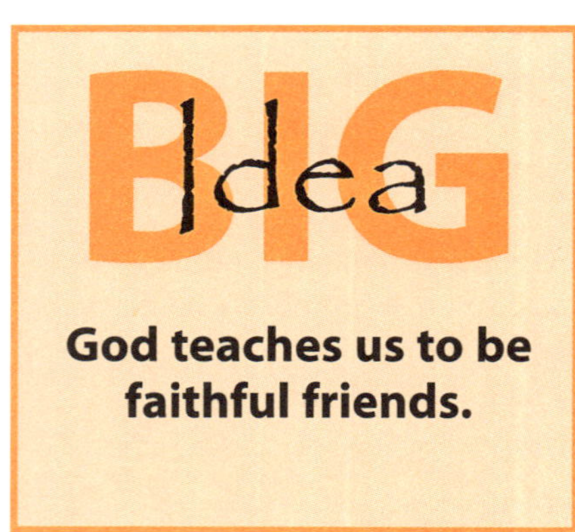

God teaches us to be faithful friends.

Session at a Glance	What You Need	What Learners Do
Ready for the Story (15 minutes)		
Welcome the Witnesses	• Poster E and Witness CD (TCK), CD player	• Review Big Ideas and read Big Idea for Session 9.
Story Warm-Up	• Posters D and P (TCK), Activity Card A (TCK), Faith Trait stickers (LR), the learners' copies of the Little Book of Faith Traits	• Review Faith Traits from Session 1-8, and learn the Faith Trait for this session: *loyalty*.
Story Fire-Up	• Chalkboard and chalk or chart paper and marker	• Brainstorm what makes a good friend.
Explore the Story (20 minutes)		
Story Set-Up	• Leaflet 9 (LR), colored pencils, Bibles	• Discover characteristics of being a good friend.
Storytelling	• Leaflet 9 (LR), Bibles	• Read the Bible story about Ruth and Naomi.
Story Follow-Up	• Leaflet 9 (LR)	• Complete a friendship activity.
Live the Story (25 minutes)		
Ways to Witness	• Poster H (TCK)	• Talk about friendship situations.
Kids Create	• One 9" x 12" (23 cm x 30 cm) piece of burlap per learner, tapestry needles, yarn, scissors, fine-tipped markers • 1" x 8" (2.5 cm x 20 cm) construction paper strips, markers, transparent tape	• Make a Friendship Saying or Friendship Chain.
Wrapping It Up	• Poster H (TCK), Leaflet 9 (LR)	• Review the Bible story and Witness Words. Pray for friends.

LR = Learner Resource
TCK = Teacher Class Kit
M&P = Materials and Preparation

Bible Background

What Factors Shaped This Story?

"The days when the judges ruled" (1:1) were difficult. The people who worshiped the Lord were unfaithful, fought among themselves, and experienced oppression from other peoples. Where could faithfulness be found? The story of Ruth is one of faithfulness in a context where women's lives and actions were not usually retold. Women were seen and defined primarily in their relationships to men. Whose daughter, wife, sister, or mother a woman was defined who she was. Family relationships were the basis of identity and entitlement to property and position.

What Is This Story About?

Having married and left their parents' homes, Naomi, Orpah, and Ruth were identified in relationship to their husbands. When the men died, the women faced crises of identity as well as economics. Respectable women were not on their own; how could they remain integrated in the web of social relationships? They could not provide for themselves; in what relationships could they find what they needed? Naomi resolved that each should return to her home. Orpah agreed but Ruth resisted. She remained with Naomi. They returned together to Bethlehem, Naomi and Elimelech's home.

In Bethlehem they were greeted with some astonishment. What will become of them? Perhaps we have a hint of the possibilities in the change from Bethlehem being a place of famine (1:1) to being a place where the barley harvest was about to begin (1:22).

Why Is This Story Important?

Faithfulness to God is realized in our faithfulness to other people. Faithfulness in relationships with other people takes us beyond the boundaries of gender roles, language, nationality, ethnicity, and family status and conventions. Ruth, a Moabite and not born of the people of ancient Israel, bound herself in faithful relationship. Her descendants include ancient Israel's King David and Jesus (Matthew 1:5, 6, 17). The book of Ruth shows that faithfulness takes us beyond the bounds of family conventions. It also shows how intimate, familial relationships can take on historical significance.

Age-Level Connection

Grade school children are tuned in to friendship. Although with younger children it sometimes seems that friendships change from week to week, it is important that 9- and 10-year-olds feel they have lasting friends and that they fit in somewhere! Hopefully, your Sunday school classroom is a place where all learners feel welcomed, accepted, and loved.

Teacher Prayer

Thank you, Jesus, for showing me how to be a faithful friend. Help me value the friendships you place in my life. Make me aware of the other Sunday school teachers and leaders, and show me how to reach out to them in friendship. Amen

Question for Reflection

How do you nurture the friendships in your life?

Learner Goals

KNOW

the friendship story of Ruth and Naomi

GROW

in understanding the importance of loyalty in their friendships

SHOW

the characteristics of a faithful friend

FACTOID

Bethlehem means "house of bread." *Elimelech* means "my God is king." *Naomi* means "pleasant." *Mara* means "bitter." *Ruth* means "friendship."

Ready for the Story (15 minutes)

faithfulness, friendship

Welcome the Witnesses

M&P *Display Poster E (Teacher Class Kit). Have Track 9 on the Witness CD (TCK), "I'm Gonna Stick with You," playing as the learners arrive.*

Greet the learners and have partners read and review the Sessions 1-8 Big Ideas from Poster E. Then read together the Big Idea for today: *God teaches us to be faithful friends*. Ask volunteers to tell about a recent time when one of the Big Ideas was helpful to them, or share an example from your own life.

Story Warm-Up

M&P *Display Posters D and P (TCK). Locate Activity Card A (TCK) and Faith Trait stickers (Learner Resource). Have the learners' copies of the Little Book of Faith Traits ready (see Session 1 "Story Warm-Up").*

Ask the learner with a birthday closest to today's date to distribute the Little Book of Faith Traits and Faith Trait stickers. Review the booklet pages for Sessions 1-8, noting the Faith Traits listed on Poster D. Read together the words you have already discussed: *generosity, obedience, patience, responsibility, boldness, thankfulness*, and *perseverance*. Some of the Faith Traits are repeated, but today's Faith Trait, *loyalty*, is new. Have the learners place today's sticker on its corresponding page. **What does it mean to be loyal?** *(To be trustworthy, truthful; to stand by your friends.)* Ask a learner to place today's marker from Activity Card A on Poster P. Then collect the booklets and save them for next time.

FACTOID

The Bible explains the Moabites as remote relatives of the Israelites. Moab was the son of Lot, who was Abraham's nephew (Genesis 11:27; 19:37).

Story Fire-Up

M&P *Write, "A good friend is..." on a chalkboard or chart paper. Have chalk or a marker available.*

Direct the learners' attention to the chalkboard or chart paper. Ask a volunteer to read the heading. Have learners take turns writing words under the heading that describe a good friend *(nice, fun, trustworthy, helpful)*. Talk about the words the learners wrote and ask if everyone agrees that they describe a good friend. Next, ask the group to discuss the list and choose the top three qualities of a good friend. Circle the group's choices. Discuss any current television shows, movies, or books that reflect these good friendship qualities.

Transition Tip

Gather in a circle. Toss a small ball randomly around the circle. The person who catches the ball completes the phrase, "A good friend is _______."

Explore the Story (20 minutes)

Story Set-Up

M&P *Have Leaflet 9 (LR), pencils, colored pencils, and Bibles available.* Have a volunteer distribute the leaflets. Ask everyone to find "Words to Live By" on page 1. Give them time to find the hidden words. *(Answers: Friendship, faithfulness.)* Do the hidden words appear on the chart the learners created earlier? (See "Story Fire-Up.") Do either of the hidden words match the top three friendship qualities the class chose? Next, have the learners use their Bibles to complete the "Friendly Proverbs" activity on page 1. Explain that the book of Proverbs contains many wise and thoughtful sayings. Proverbs is found near the middle of the Bible. Give the learners time to complete the activity, then ask several learners to share their summaries with the class.

Form three groups. Assign each group one of the situations on page 3 of the leaflet. Have the groups plan a skit depicting their assigned situation and a friendly conclusion.

Storytelling

M&P *Have Leaflet 9 (LR), pencils, and Bibles available.* Read through the Bible Text, Big Idea, and Key Verse on page 2 of the leaflet. Have everyone find Ruth 1:1-22 in their Bibles. Ask volunteers to take turns reading the passage aloud. Then look over the story scenes on page 2 of the leaflet and read the captions that accompany them. Let the learners complete the conversation balloons that appear with each scene, writing what the characters may have said. Then have several learners share the conversations they created for each story scene.

Gather the group in a circle of chairs. Stand at the center of the circle and call out a friendly trait ("Blue eyes!" "Red socks!" "Has a sister!"). Those learners who share the trait must exchange chairs. You also try to sit in a chair. The player left without a chair is the new friendly caller.

Story Follow-Up

M&P *Have Leaflet 9 (LR) and pencils available.* **Ruth's friendship with Naomi is a great example for all of us. But sometimes it isn't easy to like, much less love, some people. Are there people it is hard for you to like or love?** Allow time for thoughtful sharing and discussion. Then have learners find "What Would You Do?" on page 3 of the leaflet. Ask volunteers to read aloud each friendship situation. Let each learner complete the activity, then discuss what they could do to reflect kindness and caring in each situation.

Teacher Boost

Your friendly greeting as learners arrive for class, as well as your sincere "goodbye" as they leave, helps create a setting that learners want to return to again and again.

Witnesses in the World

Does your church have a partnership with an assisted care facility, a daycare center, or another community agency? Find out if you and your class can provide artwork or decorations for a special event the church is hosting.

Go Global!

Read the Go Global! activity on Reproducible Sheets S and T (TCK). See page 3.

GREAT good byes

Have cheerful music playing as the learners leave today. Give each a sincere smile and say, "*(Name)*, I'm glad you are my friend!"

Live the Story (25 minutes)

Ways to Witness

M&P *Display Poster H (TCK).*

Ask the learners if they have ever moved to a new town, neighborhood, church, or school. **Was it easy to make new friends? Why or why not?** *(Answers will vary.)* Ask them to pretend someone they know is moving. What advice would they give this person about making new friends? What advice would they give to the new people this person meets? Direct the group's attention to Poster H. Talk about the friendship situations depicted there. Have any of the learners been in similar situations? Ask them to share their experiences with the group.

Kids Create

M&P *For Friendship Sayings: Have a piece of 9" x 12" (23 cm x 30 cm) burlap, tapestry needle, yarn, scissors, and fine-tipped marker for each learner. For Friendship Chain: Cut assorted colors of construction paper into 1" x 8" (2.5 cm x 20 cm) strips. Have markers and transparent tape available. If you plan to make this a congregational project, write a description of the activity for a worship folder or church newsletter. Make a sample of the project you choose.*

Friendship Sayings: Show learners the sample you made. Share ideas for possible friendship phrases, such as "Friends are fun!" or "Jesus is my friend." Show the learners how to write their phrase lightly on burlap using a felt-tipped marker. Help them thread yarn through a tapestry needle and knot the end. Show them how to sew over their phrase, reminding them not to pull the yarn too tightly or the burlap will pucker. For a finishing touch, show them how to make a running stitch around the edge of the burlap.

Friendship Chain: Distribute the paper strips and markers. Have each learner write his or her name on a paper strip and then link it with the other learners' strips, creating a chain. Fasten one end of the chain to a wall or bulletin board in a hallway or fellowship area. If possible, invite other Sunday school classes to add to the Friendship Chain. Consider making this a congregational project, providing slips of paper for members to add to the chain.

Wrapping It Up

M&P *Display Poster H (TCK). Have Leaflet 9 (LR) available.*

Have the learners collect their leaflets, Bibles, and completed projects to take home. If you are working on a Friendship Chain (See "Kids Create"), have learners take paper strips home for family members and friends. Look at the Witness Words on page 4 of the leaflet and ask learners to tell how they relate to today's Bible story. Encourage everyone to share the activities on page 4 with their families. Gather around Poster H and invite the learners to add their friends' names to the closing prayer: **Thank you, God, for blessing us with friends! Today we especially thank you for** *(learners add friends' names).* **Keep showing us ways to be faithful friends! Amen**

God Calls Samuel

Session at a Glance	What You Need	What Learners Do
Ready for the Story (15 minutes)		
Welcome the Witnesses	• Poster E and Witness CD (TCK), CD player	• Review Big Ideas and discuss the Big Idea for Session 10.
Story Warm-Up	• Posters D and P (TCK), Activity Card A (TCK), Faith Trait stickers (LR), the learners' copies of the Little Book of Faith Traits	• Discuss today's Faith Trait: *honesty*.
Story Fire-Up	• Nothing	• Play a game of "Telephone."
Explore the Story (20 minutes)		
Story Set-Up	• Leaflet 10 (LR), crayons or colored pencils	• Complete a dot-to-dot puzzle.
Storytelling	• Witness CD (TCK), Leaflet 10 (LR), CD player	• Listen to the Bible story of God's call to Samuel and read a script.
Story Follow-Up	• Activity Card B2 (TCK), Bibles, reusable adhesive putty or thumbtacks	• Review the Bible story with picture sequence cards.
Live the Story (25 minutes)		
Ways to Witness	• Leaflet 10 (LR), chalk board and chalk or chart paper and marker	• Discover a special message. Think about places they serve God.
Kids Create	• potting soil, small plastic containers or flower pots, flower or vegetable seeds, water mister, index cards, fine-tipped markers, craft sticks, glue • Large paper clips, poster board, paper punch, markers	• Plant a Faith Trait Garden or make a "God Calls My Name" Mobile.
Wrapping It Up	• Poster K (TCK), Leaflet 10 (LR)	• Talk about the Witness Words and pray together.

Bible Text

1 Samuel 3:1-18

Key Verse

Speak, LORD, for your servant is listening. 1 Samuel 3:9

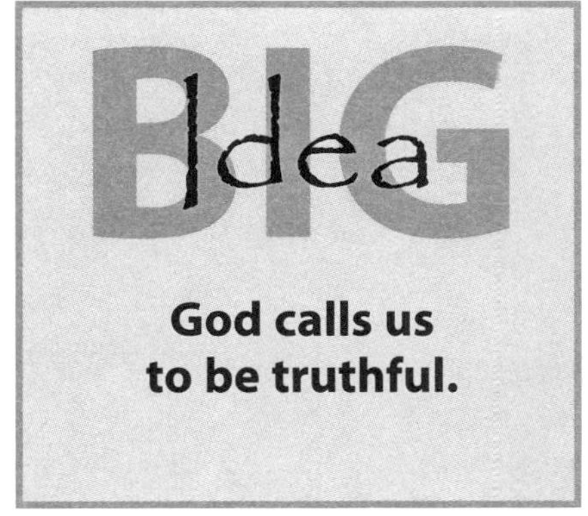

LR = Learner Resource
TCK = Teacher Class Kit
M&P = Materials and Preparation

Teacher Prayer

Jesus, I know you have called me by name, and I belong to you. Forgive me for the times when I ignore your voice. Help me to be a better listener, and show me how to respond when you call. Amen

Question for Reflection

How has God called you this week?

Learner Goals

KNOW
the story of Samuel, called by God

GROW
in confidence that they are also called by God

SHOW
thoughtfulness through serving God and others

FACTOID

The Ark of the Covenant in the temple was the symbol of God's presence on earth. The Ark, in some accounts, contained the tablets of the Ten Commandments.

Bible Background

What Factors Shaped This Story?

The child Samuel was an answer to the prayers of Hannah, who had been unable to bear children. Hannah promised that if God gave her a son she would set him apart for service to God. When Samuel was weaned, Hannah took him to Eli, the priest at Shiloh, who became Samuel's guardian and teacher. Eli's own sons stole from those who came to worship at Shiloh. Eli's sons would not inherit a priestly role. Rather, God would raise up another to be a faithful priest in Samuel.

What Is This Story About?

Three times in the night the Lord called Samuel and Samuel mistook the voice of God for that of Eli, his guardian and teacher. Eli discerned that it was God who called Samuel. Eli turned Samuel's attention to God's calling of him and instructed him how to respond. The fourth time God called, Samuel responded as he had been told: "Speak, for your servant is listening" (3:10). God told Samuel of God's plan against Eli's sons for their sins against God. Samuel lay awake with this knowledge till morning, afraid to tell Eli. But the Lord had warned Eli that this would come (2:27-36). When Samuel told Eli everything, Eli responded, "It is the Lord" (3:18), and he knew that the Lord would do what was said.

Why Is This Story Important?

God's call is not always easy to discern. We hear and recognize it with the help of others who recognize that God has purpose for us, help us listen, and teach us to respond. God has a purpose for each of us. Once we respond, God's call is not always easy to follow. We may be called to tasks we never imagined. We may be called to proclaim an unpopular message. We may be called to reform and transform the teachings and institutions that were the basis of our own education in the faith. We can follow, trusting that when God calls God also makes provision for us.

Age-Level Connection

Learners may wonder why Samuel heard the audible voice of God, but they have not. Help them understand that we hear God's voice in many different ways—through the Bible, caregivers, church leaders, and even from an "inner voice." This story is reassuring in that God values the faith of young people. God calls 9- and 10-year-olds to serve as well as adults.

Ready for the Story (15 minutes)

Welcome the Witnesses

M&P *Display Poster E (Teacher Class Kit). Have songs from the Witness CD (TCK) playing as learners arrive.*

Gather around Poster E and read the Sessions 1-9 Big Ideas together. Share the Big Idea for Session 10: *God calls us to be truthful.* **It can hurt when someone isn't truthful with us. We can also feel badly when we aren't truthful with others.** Ask volunteers to briefly tell about some of their experiences with truthfulness. When is it most difficult to be truthful?

Story Warm-Up

M&P *Display Posters D and P (TCK). Locate Activity Card A (TCK) and Faith Trait stickers (Learner Resource). Have the learners' copies of the Little Book of Faith Traits available (see Session 1 "Story Warm-Up").*

Have a volunteer locate today's Faith Trait on Poster D (*honesty*). **Being honest is another way of being truthful. Today we'll learn that God calls us to be truthful.** Have a volunteer distribute copies of the Little Book of Faith Traits and Faith Trait stickers. Have the learners place today's sticker on its corresponding page. Then ask a learner to place today's marker from Activity Card A on Poster P. Note how the markers are filling up the poster. **We are learning so much about being God's faithful witnesses!** Collect and save the booklets for next time.

Story Fire-Up

M&P *Nothing.*

Invite the learners to play a game of "Telephone." Begin by whispering "God calls us to be truthful" to the learner on your right. He or she then whispers the message to the next learner, and so on, until the message is passed around the circle. Have the last learner who receives the message say it aloud. Did the message change? Try the game a few more times, allowing the learners to create new messages. Challenge the group to listen carefully in order to keep the message from changing. After the game, talk about how difficult it can be to know if a message we hear is correct or not, especially if it has come to us through many different people. **Sometimes, even without meaning to, people change a message so it becomes untruthful. It's important for everyone to listen carefully. That is a skill Samuel learns in today's Bible story.**

respond, loyalty

FACTOID

Lord represents four Hebrew letters *hwhy*, transliterated YHWH and pronounced Yahweh (yaw-way), which is the name God told to Moses in Exodus 3:14.

 **Transition Tip** 

Ask learners to think of a favorite Bible verse or story and share it with a friend. Then have them trade places with that friend.

Talk with the learners about places or situations in which God calls us. Have them draw their ideas and post them around the classroom as a reminder that we are all called.

Invite small groups to dramatize the story of Samuel. Allow time for each group to prepare. Provide simple props such as blankets and pillows. Allow time for each group to present its drama to the rest of the class.

Explore the Story (20 minutes)

Story Set-Up

M&P *Have Leaflet 10 (LR), pencils, and crayons or colored pencils available.*

Without speaking, communicate to several learners that you want them to distribute today's learner leaflets, pencils, and coloring supplies. Then indicate silently that everyone should find "Hearing God's Call" on page 1 of the leaflet. When everyone has understood your message, say: **Thanks for being good "listeners!" Let's continue to listen carefully as we work through this activity.** After reading through the directions, invite learners to complete the dot-to-dot puzzle and then color it in. As they are working, talk about the story of Jonah. When God called Jonah, Jonah disobeyed God and went the other way! But in the end, Jonah listened to God and shared the message God had given him.

Storytelling

M&P *Have Track 10 of the Witness CD (TCK) ready to play. Have Leaflet 10 (LR) available.*

Ask a volunteer to read aloud the Bible Text, Big Idea, and Key Verse on page 2 of the leaflet. Then invite the learners to listen carefully to the story of God calling Samuel as you play Track 10 on the Witness CD, "Wake Up Call." After listening to the story, direct the group's attention to "Samuel Hears God's Call" on page 2. Ask volunteers to read the parts of the Narrator, Samuel, Eli, and the voice of God. Give the readers time to look over the script and then ask them to gather at the front of your classroom as they read their parts aloud while the other learners follow along. Then thank the learners who read the script and ask them to return to their seats.

Story Follow-Up

M&P *Prepare Activity Card B2 (TCK). Have Bibles and reusable adhesive putty or thumbtacks available.*

Distribute the prepared activity cards to volunteers, perhaps those who did not have speaking parts for the script presented earlier. Ask the learners to stand in order so that their cards retell the story of Samuel. Encourage the group to offer help as needed, referring to 1 Samuel 3:1-18 in their Bibles. After the learners are in correct order, have them display the cards on a wall or bulletin board. Discuss how Samuel may have felt when he realized that it was God, not Eli, calling him. **How would you have felt if you had been Samuel?** *(Answers will vary.)*

Live the Story (25 minutes)

Ways to Witness

M&P *Have Leaflet 10 (LR), pencils, chalkboard and chalk or chart paper and marker available.*
Ask the learners to find "Picture Puzzle" on page 3 in their leaflets. Working with a partner, have the learners complete the activity. *(Answer: Here I am, for you called me.)* Ask a volunteer to write this special message on a chalkboard or chart paper. Then continue with "Serving God" on page 3 of the leaflet. Have the learners write a description or draw a picture that tells about a place and way they serve God. Invite learners to share their completed activity with the class. **When we serve others, we are answering God's call.**

Kids Create

M&P *For Faith Trait Garden: Gather potting soil, small plastic containers (such as yogurt containers) or small flowerpots, flower or vegetable seeds, water mister, index cards, fine-tipped markers, craft sticks, and glue. For "God Calls My Name" Mobile: Have large paper clips, markers, and 4" x 4" (10 cm x 10 cm) squares of poster board with a hole punched through the top and bottom of each square (one square for each letter in each learner's first name). Make a sample of the project you choose.*
Faith Trait Garden: Planting and caring for seeds can remind learners that God cares for us as we grow. Have learners fill plastic containers half full of potting soil. Add a few seeds. Gently cover the seeds with soil and then mist with water. Make flags from index cards that say, "Watch me grow!" Suggest learners add their favorite Faith Trait to their flag. Glue the flag to the end of a craft stick and place it carefully in the soil. Keep the pots in a sunny classroom window, or invite the learners to care for them at home.
"God Calls My Name" Mobile: Show the learners a sample mobile. Give each learner enough poster board squares to spell out his or her first name. Let them use markers to print one letter of their name on both sides of each square, decorating them as they wish. Next, show them how to join the squares together using paper clips. Add a paper clip to the top of the completed mobile for hanging. Suspend the mobiles in your classroom, or invite the learners to display them at home.

Wrapping It Up

M&P *Display Poster K (TCK). Have Leaflet 10 (LR) available.*
Have the learners collect their leaflets, Bibles, and completed projects to take home. Find Witness Words on page 4 of the leaflet and ask learners to tell how the words relate to today's Bible story. Look through the activities on page 4 and remind learners to try them with their families. Ask them to tell about past activities they tried. Gather around Poster K. Ask a volunteer to read the caption on the poster. Remind the learners that God calls us to be truthful. Ask volunteers to begin and end a prayer. Invite the other learners to add their own prayers in between. Close the prayer with a big "Amen!"

Teacher Boost

Using a person's name is a way of showing care and respect. Taking time to call upon your learners by name helps them feel important to you.

Witnesses in the World

Volunteers help keep a church running! Learn about some of the tasks volunteers do in your church, such as addressing envelopes, yard work, and cleaning. Create a "thank you" bulletin board, honoring those who help make your church a great place to witness to God's love!

Give each learner a sincere and honest compliment as he or she leaves today. Remind them that God calls us to be truthful every day.

David and Goliath

Bible Text

1 Samuel 17:4-11, 32-50

Key Verse

David said, "The LORD, who saved me from the paw of the lion and the paw of the bear, will save me from the hand of this Philistine."
1 Samuel 17:37

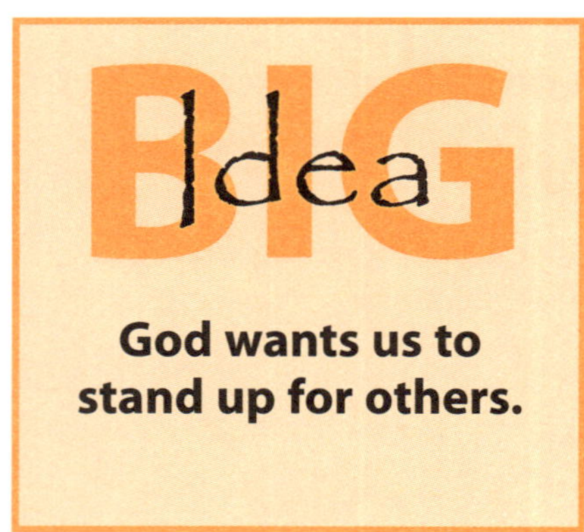

God wants us to stand up for others.

Session at a Glance	What You Need	What Learners Do
Ready for the Story (15 minutes)		
Welcome the Witnesses	• Poster E and Witness CD (TCK), CD player	• Review Big Ideas and discuss the Big Idea for Session 11.
Story Warm-Up	• Posters D and P (TCK), Activity Card A (TCK), Faith Trait stickers, the learners' copies of the Little Book of Faith Traits	• Review Faith Traits for Sessions 1-10, and learn the Faith Trait for this session: *responsibility*.
Story Fire-Up	• Poster I (TCK), popcorn, small bags or bowls	• Enjoy a "theater" introduction to the Bible story.
Explore the Story (20 minutes)		
Story Set-Up	• Leaflet 11 (LR), rulers, yard or meter sticks, tape measures, calculator	• Compare Biblical measurements to measurements we use today.
Storytelling	• Poster I and Witness CD (TCK), Leaflet 11 (LR), CD player	• Listen to the Bible story about David and Goliath.
Story Follow-Up	• Activity Cards C1 and C2 (TCK)	• Review and retell the Bible story.
Live the Story (25minutes)		
Ways to Witness	• Leaflet 11 (LR)	• Discover the names of some of God's faithful witnesses.
Kids Create	• "Y"-shaped branches, assorted strings and yarns • Clean, smooth stones, craft paint, paintbrushes, clear-drying sealer, water, paper toweling	• Create a Slingshot Weaving or Painted Stones.
Wrapping It Up	• Witness CD (TCK), Leaflet 11 (LR), CD player	• Review the Witness Words. Pray together.

LR = Learner Resource
TCK = Teacher Class Kit
M&P = Materials and Preparation

Bible Background

What Factors Shaped This Story?

Under Samuel's leadership the ancient Israelites demanded from God a king like the other nations. The first king was Saul whom Samuel anointed, but Saul proved unworthy. The Lord sent Samuel to the house of Jesse in Bethlehem, where Samuel would find the new king. That king was David, a shepherd and Jesse's youngest son. The story of David and Goliath is that of David's first military victory.

What Is This Story About?

Imagine the biggest, most heavily armed, most powerful and frightening warrior you can. That was Goliath the Philistine. He was almost 10 feet (3 meters) tall. Goliath challenged the Israelites to send someone to do battle with him. Whoever won the fight would make servants of the opponent's people. The Israelites quaked with fear.

David was young and not the most experienced, but he volunteered. He figured that if he could protect the sheep from lions and bears, he could handle Goliath. David trusted that God would protect him as God had done in the past. Unaccustomed to military armor and weaponry, David went in his shepherd's garb and with his shepherd's staff and bag, in which he placed five stones for use in his slingshot—hardly an adequate weapon against Goliath. Goliath came to do battle with David, who drew out his slingshot, hit Goliath square in the forehead, and won the battle.

Why Is This Story Important?

What is the source of real power? We tend to think that military might, wealth, and political power rule the world. None of these amounts to anything beside the power of God on which David relied. This story is not so much about God taking up arms against human beings as it is about the real nature of power. God stands with those who appear to be weak and brings to naught those who wield the power of this world.

Age-Level Connection

Third and fourth graders know all too well what it feels like to be small and powerless. They sometimes feel that older youth and adults don't listen to them or respect their ideas or opinions. In the story of David and Goliath, David trusts God to make him strong. Through David, other people see that all power belongs to God.

Teacher Prayer

Thank you, Lord, for walking with me throughout this week. When I feel powerless, help me to remember that you are the true source of all power. Thank you for caring for me always. Amen

Question for Reflection

How have you experienced God's faithfulness in your life?

Learner Goals

KNOW
the story of David and Goliath

GROW
in understanding that God gives us courage to act responsibly

SHOW
basic knowledge of Biblical measurements, including *span* and *cubit*

FACTOID

A cubit, about 17½" (44 centimeters), equals two spans. A span is three handbreadths. A handbreadth is four fingers. Some say a cubit equals seven (rather than six) handbreadths.

Witness WORDS

anointed, cubit, span

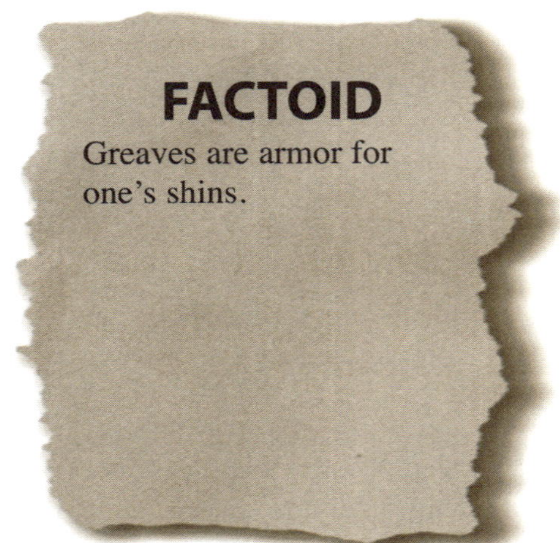

FACTOID

Greaves are armor for one's shins.

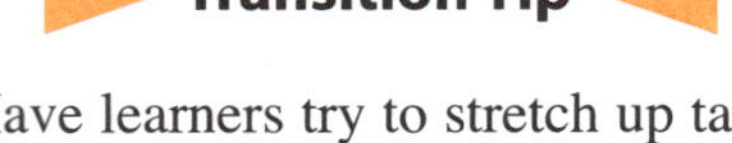

Transition Tip

Have learners try to stretch up tall, like Goliath, crouch down small, like a stone, and then stretch side to side before continuing with the session.

Ready for the Story (15 minutes)

Welcome the Witnesses

M&P *Display Poster E (Teacher Class Kit). Have songs from the Witness CD (TCK) playing as learners arrive.*

Ask learners to name Big Ideas you have learned so far, without looking at Poster E. Then review the Sessions 1-10 Big Ideas using the poster. Read today's Big Idea together *(God wants us to stand up for others)*. Ask volunteers to tell about times they stood up for someone who was being treated unkindly by others. Share a story of your own.

Story Warm-Up

M&P *Display Poster D and P (TCK). Locate Activity Card A (TCK), and Faith Trait stickers (LR). Have available the learners' copies of the Little Book of Faith Traits (see Session 1 "Story Warm-Up").*

Distribute the Little Book of Faith Traits to the learners and let them read through the Faith Trait words they've already added to their booklets: *generosity, obedience, patience, responsibility, boldness, thankfulness, perseverance, obedience, loyalty,* and *honesty*. The Faith Trait word for today is *responsibility*. Have the learners place today's Faith Trait sticker in their booklets and find today's Faith Trait on Poster D. Then ask a volunteer to place today's marker from Activity Card A on Poster P. **What does it mean to be responsible?** *(To be trustworthy, to do what's right.)* Collect and save the booklets for next time.

Story Fire-Up

M&P *Display Poster I (TCK). Have popcorn ready to serve in small paper bags or bowls. Before serving any food, always check with caregivers for learners who have food allergies. Provide an alternative, if necessary.*

Call attention to Poster I. **Where have you seen posters similar to this one?** *(At a movie theater.)* Ask a learner to help you distribute the popcorn and invite everyone to enjoy a snack together. As you eat the popcorn, talk about how exciting it is to see a movie where the good guy or girl wins. Ask the learners to share examples of their favorite movies in which the hero succeeds or wins at something. Tell the learners that today's Bible story is about David and Goliath. Invite learners to tell what they know about this story. **Be on the lookout for several Faith Traits in today's story, including *obedience, loyalty,* and *responsibility*.**

Explore the Story (20 minutes)

Story Set-Up

M&P *Have Leaflet 11 (LR) ready. Locate common measuring tools including rulers, yard or meter sticks, and tape measures. Bring along a calculator.*

Distribute the measuring tools. **These are some of the measurement tools we use today. In Bible times, people had a different way of measuring.** Ask a volunteer to distribute the learner leaflets. Have everyone find "A Different Way to Measure" on page 1. After reading through the introduction, look through the "Common Biblical Measurement Chart" and then invite partners to complete the activity together, helping them with the multiplication problems as needed. Afterward, have partners share what they discovered with the class. Emphasize that knowing a little about Bible times measurements helps us better understand the story of David and Goliath.

Storytelling

M&P *Be ready to refer to Poster I (TCK) that you displayed earlier. Have Track 11 of the Witness CD (TCK) ready to play. Have Leaflet 11 (LR) and pencils ready.*

Point out the difference in David and Goliath's size on Poster I and in the illustration on page 2 of the learner leaflet. Ask a volunteer to read aloud the Bible Text, Big Idea, and Key Verse that appear on page 2. Invite the learners to listen to "Todd's Tall Tale," Track 11 on the Witness CD. Then return to page 2 of the leaflet and read through the instructions for completing "With Only a Slingshot." Give learners time to number the story scenes in correct order and write a caption for each one.

Story Follow-Up

M&P *Locate and prepare Activity Cards C1 and C2 (TCK).*

Show learners the activity cards you have prepared, creating David and Goliath masks. Ask two learners to wear the masks as they retell the story, using voices and actions to portray each of the characters. If you have time, let other pairs of learners retell the story in this way.

Name activities in which the learners are responsible, such as playing on a sports team, serving as a school crossing guard, and playing a musical instrument. How are they responsible in each activity? When is it difficult? How can God help?

Use sidewalk chalk or masking tape to create a hopscotch game on a sidewalk, hallway, or the classroom floor. Write or tape a Faith Trait word in each box. Use small stones or beanbags as markers. Have learners call out each Faith Trait as they hop on it!

Teacher Boost

Each time you ask a learner to help with a classroom task or affirm him or her during the session, you are making that learner feel special and needed.

Witnesses in the World

An advocate is someone who speaks up for others. Does your church support an advocacy program, such as a foster care or world hunger program? Utilize the creativity of your learners by making and displaying posters in support of such programs.

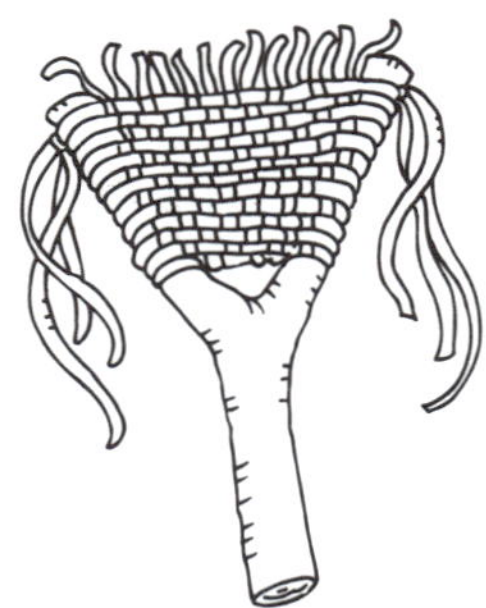

Play praise music as the learners leave today. Whisper a special message to each child that reflects how much God loves him or her.

Live the Story (25 minutes)

Ways to Witness

M&P *Have Leaflet 11 (LR) and pencils ready.*

Ask the learners to find page 3 in their leaflets. Have a volunteer read aloud the introduction to "People of God." Then give the learners time to unscramble the letters to reveal the names of faithful Bible people they have learned about this semester *(Answers: Abraham, Sarah, Moses, Samuel, Noah, Gideon, Eli, Hannah, Ruth, Naomi, and Joshua)*. Encourage them to add the scrambled names of people they know who are faithful today, and then have partners try to unscramble them. If time permits, ask the learners to tell why the people they named are faithful witnesses.

Kids Create

M&P *For Slingshot Weaving: Have a "Y"-shaped branch for each learner, assorted colors of string or yarn, and scissors. For Painted Stones: Have clean, smooth stones, craft paints, paintbrushes, clear-drying sealer (available at craft stores), water, and paper toweling for clean-up. Make a sample of the project you choose.*

Slingshot Weaving: Show the learners a sample "Slingshot Weaving." Demonstrate how to tie a strand of string or yarn to the base of one of the "Y" arms on a branch and then wrap the strand back and forth around both arms, creating a surface on which to weave. Tie off the strand and trim the end. Then show the learners how to weave in and out with assorted strings and yarns to make a pleasing pattern.

Painted Stones: Show the learners a completed project. Give each learner a stone and paints. Let them paint a design on the stone that will remind them to be a faithful follower of God, such as a cross or David's shepherding crook. Suggest that they include the reference of a favorite Bible verse or a Faith Trait word. After the stones are painted, allow them to dry and then have the learners paint over them with a clear-drying sealer.

Wrapping It Up

M&P *Have the Witness CD (TCK), Leaflet 11 (LR), and a CD player available.*

Play songs from the Witness CD as the learners clean up the class area. Have them collect their leaflets, Bibles, and completed projects to take home. Find the Witness Words on page 4 of the leaflet and discuss their meaning. Remind learners to try the activities on page 4 with their families. Ask the learners to join you in prayer: **Thank you, God, for the story of David and Goliath. Help us remember that no matter how big or small we are, or what skills or experiences we have in life, you give us the ability to live as your faithful, responsible followers. Amen**

Daniel in the Lions' Den

Session at a Glance	What You Need	What Learners Do
Ready for the Story (15 minutes)		
Welcome the Witnesses	• Poster E and Witness CD (TCK), CD player	• Review Big Ideas and discuss the Big Idea for Session 12.
Story Warm-Up	• Posters D and P (TCK), Activity Card A (TCK), Faith Trait stickers (LR), the learners' copies of the Little Book of Faith Traits	• Review Faith Traits for Sessions 1-11, and learn today's Faith Trait: *honesty*.
Story Fire-Up	• Poster J (TCK), large mixing bowl and spoon, a variety of snack foods, paper cups	• Make and enjoy a snack together.
Explore the Story (20 minutes)		
Story Set-Up	• Leaflet 12 (LR), Bibles, gummy worms, paper bag	• Talk about trust. Learn about Bible people who trusted God.
Storytelling	• Witness CD (TCK), Leaflet 12 (LR), CD player	• Talk about the Bible story and sing a song.
Story Follow-Up	• Leaflet 12 (LR)	• Learn about different types of prayer.
Live the Story (25 minutes)		
Ways to Witness	• Nothing	• Pantomime ways we show faith.
Kids Create	• Poster board, drawing paper, yarn or ribbon, paper punch, scissors, markers, crayons • One cotton gardening glove per learner, felt scraps, fabric glue, fine-tipped permanent markers	• Make a Prayer Journal or a "Daniel and the Lions" Glove Puppet.
Wrapping It Up	• Posters I and J (TCK), Witness CD (TCK), Leaflet 12 (LR), CD player	• Review the Witness Words. Pray together.

Bible Text

Daniel 6

Key Verse

I make a decree, that in all my royal dominion people should tremble and fear before the God of Daniel: For he is the living God, enduring forever. Daniel 6:26

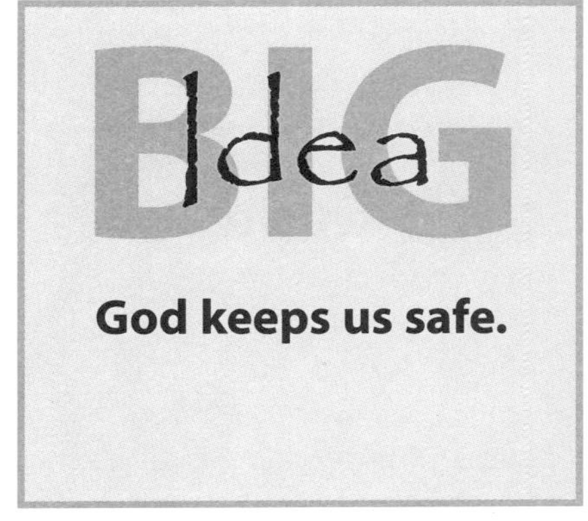

LR = Learner Resource
TCK = Teacher Class Kit
M&P = Materials and Preparation

Teacher Prayer

Spirit of Life, you have created a wonderful world. Thank you! Help me find ways every day to stop and appreciate your greatness, especially in the small things I notice around me. Amen

Question for Reflection

How can you have a more meaningful prayer life? Consider the value of keeping a prayer journal.

Learner Goals

KNOW
the story of Daniel trusting God

GROW
in faith that God will keep us safe

SHOW
understanding of the importance of daily prayer and the many ways we can pray

FACTOID

Darius planned to appoint Daniel over the satraps, who governed the empire's provinces. Each had a military and a civil leader serving under the satrap.

Bible Background

What Factors Shaped This Story?

The book of Daniel was written to encourage the people of God when they were oppressed and exploited. The first six chapters tell six stories of the faithful young Daniel. He and others faced repeated persecutions. Each time God rescued them. These stories referred to the people's past in exile. Chapters 7–12 tell four stories to address more contemporary persecutions that the people suffered under the Greek imperial occupation of their land. Antiochus IV Epiphanes was a brutal ruler intent on turning Jerusalem from a holy place for the people of God into a monument to the Greek gods. The stories again teach that God is sovereign and will protect and deliver the people.

What Is This Story About?

Daniel was the most excellent among King Darius's administrators. Darius planned to give him the highest position, and the other administrators became jealous. Daniel was also a pious person and faithful to God. The other administrators tried to use Daniel's faithfulness against him. They came to Darius proposing a new ordinance that no one should pray—except to Darius—for 30 days. They said that all his administrators were in favor. They were lying, of course, since Daniel knew nothing of this. No doubt flattered, Darius signed the ordinance. Daniel didn't comply because of his faithfulness to God. The conspirators wanted Daniel thrown to the lions. Darius was powerless to rescue Daniel, even though Darius himself put the ordinance into effect. That didn't matter because God was faithful to Daniel and protected him in the lions' den. Daniel's enemies were thrown into the lions' den, and Darius became a worshiper of Daniel's God.

Why Is This Story Important?

Daniel's faithfulness was used against him. God was faithful to Daniel and protected him. Acting on his faith was Daniel's witness to Darius, who saw the power of God to save. The power of kings is finally subject to the power of God.

Age-Level Connection

Daniel and the lions is a favorite Bible story for many children. Even when faced with a night in the lions' den, Daniel's trust in God did not waver. One of Daniel's greatest gifts was his faithful prayer life. The activities in today's session will help the learners realize how important it is for them to always trust in God.

Ready for the Story (15 minutes)

Welcome the Witnesses

M&P *Display Poster E (Teacher Class Kit). Have songs from the Witness CD (TCK) playing as the learners arrive.*
Have a learner find today's Big Idea on Poster E and then say it together *(God keeps us safe)*. **When you were little, what scared you?** *(Storms, dark closets.)* **What scares you now?** *(Some may express the same fears as before.)* **It's good to talk honestly about our fears and to trust that God keeps us safe.**

Story Warm-Up

M&P *Display Posters D and P (TCK). Locate Activity Card A (TCK) and Faith Trait stickers (Learner Resource). Have available the learners' copies of the Little Book of Faith Traits (see Session 1 "Story Warm-Up").*
Ask a volunteer to distribute the Little Book of Faith Traits and Faith Trait stickers. Find the page for today's Faith Trait (*honesty*) and invite the learners to add the corresponding sticker. Point to the matching image on Poster D. Then ask a learner to add today's Faith Trait marker from Activity Card A to Poster P. Take time to look through all the markers added to the poster so far, naming the Faith Traits that accompany them: *generosity, obedience, patience, responsibility, boldness, thankfulness, perseverance, obedience, loyalty, honesty, responsibility*, and *honesty*. Collect and save the booklets for next time.

Story Fire-Up

M&P *Display Poster J (TCK). Bring along a large mixing bowl, mixing spoon, and small containers of snack foods, such as pretzels, cereal loops, animal crackers, raisins, and M&Ms. Have small paper cups for serving. Before serving any food, always check with caregivers for learners who have food allergies. Provide an alternative, if necessary.*
Point to Poster J and ask the learners to tell what they know about the Bible story it portrays. **Why is *honesty* an important part of Daniel's story?** *(If learners are unsure, encourage them to keep that question in mind as you explore today's story.)*

Remind the learners of the Bible story about David and Goliath (Session 11), and how exciting it can be to watch a movie or read a book in which the good guy or girl wins. **Like David, Daniel was a courageous Bible times person who trusted God to keep him safe.** Before exploring the story, invite the learners to work together to create a "lion-sized" snack! Have them wash their hands and then pour all the ingredients you provide into a large bowl, mixing it with a spoon. Provide cups for scooping out servings of the snack mix.

honesty, witness

FACTOID

Daniel's three daily prayers would have been morning, midday, and evening. Christian tradition includes up to nine prayer times throughout the day and night.

 **Transition Tip** 

Teach learners a call and response phrase to indicate when it's time to change to a new activity. Today's phrase may be: *Leader:* "Daniel had..." *Learners:* "grrrrrrreat faith!"

Make a prayer chart. Let the learners add their prayer concerns each week. Include their concerns in your closing prayers. Provide stickers for marking answered prayers.

Get the learners moving by having them act: as quietly as a mouse, as slithery as a snake, as funny as a monkey, as slowly as a sloth, and as majestically as a lion.

Explore the Story (20 minutes)

Story Set-Up

M&P *Conceal a few gummy worms in a paper bag. Have additional gummy worms available. Locate Leaflet 12 (LR), pencils, and Bibles. Before serving any food, always check with caregivers for learners who have food allergies. Provide an alternative, if necessary.*

Show learners the paper bag you have prepared, but do not tell them what is inside it. **Do you trust me enough to reach inside this bag and touch what I've placed in it?** Invite volunteers to reach inside and then describe what the contents of the bag feels like *(squishy, slimy)*. After everyone has had an opportunity to reach inside the bag, ask learners to guess what they touched. Show the learners the gummy worms in the bag. Set the bag aside and then bring out the additional gummy worms you have and give each learner a few of them to add to their snack mix. **Was it easy to trust me? Why or why not?** *(Answers may vary.)* **Is it always easy to trust God?** *(Accept all answers.)* **Sometimes it can be hard to trust God. In today's Bible story, Daniel trusts God even though it was probably very hard to do.** Distribute the leaflets, Bibles, and pencils. Have everyone find "Trusting God" on page 1 of the leaflet. Form small groups and have them work together to complete the activity, matching the Bible verses with the pictures.

Storytelling

M&P *Have Track 12 of the Witness CD (TCK) ready to play. Have Leaflet 12 (LR) available.*

Turn to page 2 of the leaflet and ask a learner to read aloud the Bible Text, Big Idea, and Key Verse. Then take turns reading "A Man of Faith." **Why were the king's officials jealous of Daniel?** *(The king was pleased with Daniel's work; he liked Daniel.)* **How did Daniel feel about the king's new law?** *(He wanted to obey the king, but he knew it was more important to obey God.)* **In what ways was Daniel honest?** *(He didn't try to hide his faith; he let God be in charge of the situation.)* **How do you think Daniel felt when he was in the lion's den?** *(Afraid, trusting God.)* **When is it hard for you to trust God to keep you safe?** *(Accept all answers, making the point that we can trust that God is with us in any situation, even when the result isn't the one we hoped for.)* After discussing the story, listen to "Here Kitty, Kitty," Track 12 on the Witness CD. Invite the learners to sing along on the chorus!

Story Follow-Up

M&P *Have Leaflet 12 (LR) and pencils available.*

Daniel valued prayer so much he prayed three times a day. When are your favorite times to pray? *(In my bed at night; before meals; when I'm feeling afraid; when I've had a great day.)* Have the learners find "How Do You Pray?" on page 3 of their leaflets. Read through the introduction together. Share ideas for praying the different types of prayers listed. Then give the learners time to work independently as they write their own prayers to God. Let them know you will ask volunteers to share their prayers as part of your closing time today.

Live the Story (25 minutes)

Ways to Witness

M&P *Nothing.*

How do people know we have faith in God? Invite volunteers to pantomime their ideas for the group to guess *(prayer, attending worship services, reading the Bible, singing in a church choir, helping a friend, offering a hug).* Encourage discussion about the things we say and do that reveal our faith to others.

Kids Create

M&P *For Prayer Journal: Have for each learner: Two 5" x 7" (13 cm x 18 cm) sheets of poster board, several 5" x 7" (13 cm x 18 cm) or slightly smaller sheets of drawing paper, yarn or ribbon, paper punch, scissors, markers and crayons. For "Daniel and the Lions" Glove Puppet: Have a cotton gardening glove for each learner, scissors, felt scraps, fabric glue, and fine-tipped permanent markers. Make a sample of the project you choose.*

Prayer Journal: Show learners a sample Prayer Journal. Distribute poster board and drawing paper. Show the learners how to place the paper between the pieces of poster board, creating a booklet. Help them punch holes along the left side of their booklet. Provide yarn or ribbon for lacing the booklet together. Give them time to decorate the cover as they wish. Encourage them to use their Prayer Journal each day, writing prayers or drawing pictures of prayer requests. Remind them to also offer God thanks for answered prayers.

"Daniel and the Lions" Glove Puppet: Show the learners a completed glove puppet. Then have them cut felt pieces to create Daniel, the king, and three lions. Suggest they add details to each figure using permanent markers, then glue each figure to the glove fingers. When their puppet gloves are complete, have learners take turns retelling today's Bible story. Encourage them to use their puppets to tell the story to family members at home.

Wrapping It Up

M&P *Locate Posters I and J (TCK). Have the Witness CD (TCK), Leaflet 12 (LR), and a CD player available.*

Play Track 12 from the Witness CD as the learners help clean up and collect their things. Find the Witness Words on page 4 of the leaflet and discuss how they relate to the Bible story. Remind everyone to try the activities on page 4 with their families. Display Posters I and J together as a reminder that God gives us courage to act responsibly and honestly. Gather the group together and ask volunteers to read the prayers they wrote on page 3 of their leaflets. Pray: **Mighty God, hear us as we pray...** *invite learners to share their written prayers...* **for all your gifts and so much more, we thank you! Amen**

Teacher Boost

One of the most important things you can do as a teacher is pray for your learners! Make it a regular practice to include them in your daily prayers.

Witnesses in the World

Arrange for your class to write prayers to be offered during an upcoming worship service. If learners will be offering the prayers themselves, practice saying them slowly and clearly. If possible, practice with a microphone in your church's worship space.

Go Global!

Read the Go Global! activity on Reproducible Sheets S and T (TCK). See page 3.

Play music as the learners depart. Tell them you are glad they were here and that you will be praying for them this week.

The Peaceful Kingdom

Bible Text

Isaiah 11:1-9

Key Verse

They will not hurt or destroy on all my holy mountain; for the earth will be full of the knowledge of the LORD as the waters cover the sea. Isaiah 11:9

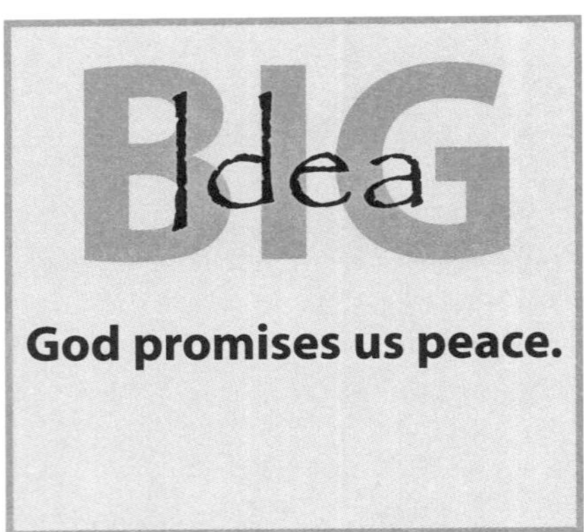

LR = Learner Resource
TCK = Teacher Class Kit
M&P = Materials and Preparation

Session at a Glance	What You Need	What Learners Do
Ready for the Story (15 minutes)		
Welcome the Witnesses	• Poster E and Witness CD (TCK), CD player	• Review Big Ideas and discuss the Big Idea for Session 13.
Story Warm-Up	• Posters D, L, and P (TCK), Activity Cards A and D (TCK), Faith Trait stickers (LR), the learners' copies of the Little Book of Faith Traits	• Learn today's Faith Trait: *peace*. Play a game.
Story Fire-Up	• Poster A and Witness CD (TCK), index cards, chalkboard and chalk or chart paper and marker	• Unscramble clues to spell PEACE.
Explore the Story (20 minutes)		
Story Set-Up	• Poster M (TCK), Leaflet 13 (LR), Bibles, world map or globe	• Talk about world peace. Define the word *prophet*.
Storytelling	• Leaflet 13 and Session 13 stickers (LR)	• Read the Bible story.
Story Follow-Up	• Reproducible Sheet E (TCK), Leaflet 13 (LR)	• Complete a crossword puzzle and make a Secret Animal Square.
Live the Story (25 minutes)		
Ways to Witness	• Miscellaneous props	• Role-play peaceful resolutions to conflict.
Kids Create	• Clean soup cans, masking tape, brown shoe polish, cleaning rags • Construction paper or card stock, ink pads, fine-tipped markers, wet paper towels	• Make a Snakeskin Pencil Holder or Fingerprint Cards.
Wrapping It Up	• Leaflet 13 (LR), Witness CD (TCK), CD player	• Review the Witness Words and pray together.

Bible Background

What Factors Shaped This Story?

The prophet Isaiah spoke during the latter eighth and early ninth centuries B.C.E. During Isaiah's time the Israelites lived under the power and threat of the Assyrian empire. There was also failure of faith and attendant injustice among the people. Isaiah foretells both of the reality of external threat and of internal threat in the people's life. Isaiah prophesies God's punishment against the people's arrogance and injustice and foretells God's deliverance of the people from their enemies. God's will is for a faithful people living in justice and peace.

What Is This Story About?

Though God seems absent when the people are rebellious and when they suffer oppression, Isaiah says that a new time will come. God will deliver them from their oppression. Their enemies will be destroyed. A child will be born the Messiah king, who will bring justice, righteousness, and peace. The Messiah will be a descendant of David and of Jesse, David's father. The spirit of the Lord will be present with this leader. The leader will have the gifts of wisdom, understanding, counsel, might, knowledge, and fear of the Lord. The leader will bring justice for the poor and meek; the wicked will be destroyed. Creation will be made new. Peace will come and be realized in all creation. Those who now seem to be "natural" enemies will live together, even sleep alongside one another in safety. They will eat together and raise their young together. All creation will know God. The knowledge of God will be as much a part of creation as water is part of the sea.

Why Is This Story Important?

There is hope. Isaiah prophesied that God protects and provides for the people against both their external enemies and their own faithlessness and rebellion. God never abandoned the ancient Israelites and will not abandon us. God brings judgment, justice, and restoration. God raises up leaders who see God's vision of wholeness.

Age-Level Connection

With the technology and media available to children today, they are in tune with much of what is going on in the world, although they may not be able to truly comprehend or understand it. Children of all ages, however, want a peaceful world. God's promise of peace is one that they can cling to throughout their lives.

Teacher Prayer

Prince of Peace, help me have a peaceful day! Focus my mind on peace as I enter my Sunday school classroom, and guide my words and actions to reflect the hope your promises bring. Amen.

Question for Reflection

How do you create peaceful moments in the midst of a busy day?

Learner Goals

KNOW

Isaiah's prophecy of a peaceful world

GROW

in understanding their role in creating peace

SHOW

a peaceful attitude in their daily lives

FACTOID

God promised that Israel's king would always come from the family of King David.

Ready for the Story (15 minutes)

prophet, justice, descendant

Welcome the Witnesses

M&P *Display Poster E (Teacher Class Kit). Have songs from the Witness CD (TCK) playing as the learners arrive.*

Greet the learners by saying, "Hi (*Name*)! God's peace to you!" Help each learner recall one of the Big Ideas you have learned so far. Then read through the Big Ideas on Poster E, concluding with "God promises us peace." **What is peace?** *(No war, a quiet place.)* **Where is your favorite peaceful place?** *(My bedroom, the park.)* **Peaceful places are a gift from God.**

Story Warm-Up

M&P *Display Posters D and P (TCK). Locate Activity Card A (TCK) and Faith Trait stickers (Learner Resource). Have ready Poster L (TCK) and Activity Card D (TCK). Have available the learners' copies of the Little Book of Faith Traits (see Session 1 "Story Warm-Up").*

Point to Poster D and say today's Faith Trait together (*peace*). Distribute the Little Book of Faith Traits and Faith Trait stickers. Have learners place today's sticker on the booklet page for this session. Then ask a learner to place today's marker from Activity Card A on Poster P. Collect and save the booklets for next time. Next, invite the learners to gather for a fun game as you place Poster L and the game cards from Activity Card D on a table or on the floor. Follow directions for playing the game, reviewing the Faith Traits you have learned.

FACTOID

The Bible does not mention the death of Isaiah, nor of any other of the prophets, maybe to show that their books are of undying relevance.

Story Fire-Up

M&P *Display Poster A (TCK). Have Track 17 ("Creature Sounds") of the Witness CD (TCK) playing quietly in the background. Bring along five index cards and a marker. Have a chalkboard and chalk or chart paper and marker available.*

Point to the animals on Poster A as the learners listen quietly to the recording of nature sounds. Then invite the learners to play a guessing game. Give clues and invite the learners to guess the animals they describe. Ask a volunteer to write the correct animal names on a chalkboard or chart paper.

Clues: I store water in a hump on my back. *(Camel.)* I slither through the ocean like an electric snake. *(Eel.)* I live in a marshy swamp and have a large jaw and bumpy skin. *(Alligator.)* I have a curly tail and I like to roll in the mud. *(Pig.)* My trunk helps me eat. *(Elephant.)* Now ask another learner to write the first letter of each name on an index card. Have the group work together to unscramble the letters, revealing a word (*peace*). **Today we will learn more about God's promise of peace.**

When the learners are getting antsy, have them trade places with someone who is the same height or who has the same eye color. This is also a fun way to choose partners for activities.

Explore the Story (20 minutes)

Story Set-Up

M&P *Display Poster M (TCK). Have Leaflet 13 (LR), pencils, and Bibles ready. Locate a world map or globe.*

Ask two learners to hold up a world map or globe so that everyone can see it. **Where is there war in the world today?** *(Help the learners locate areas of war and unrest on the map or globe.)* **Where is there peace in the world today?** *(Help the learners locate areas where they feel peace exists. Some may feel there is no place on earth where it is totally peaceful.)* Next, point to the image on Poster M. **Where might this creature live? Is there fighting or a war that might threaten its survival? How might leaders in that place help keep it safe?** *(Accept all answers.)* **God promises us peace. Could we promise peace to this imaginary animal? Why or why not?** *(Answers will vary.)* Have a volunteer distribute the leaflets and ask everyone to find "What the Bible Says About Peace" on page 1. Assign partners or small groups one or more of the verses to locate in their Bibles. Ask them to summarize their verse(s) for the class. Then continue with "What is a Prophet?" on page 1. Help the learners understand that Isaiah's message is still important for us to hear today.

Storytelling

M&P *Have Leaflet 13 and Session 13 stickers (LR) ready.*

Read together the Bible Text, Big Idea, and Key Verse on page 2 of the leaflet. Distribute the stickers to complete the page, and then ask the learners to read through the text with you. **Isaiah spoke of someone God would send to help the world live in peace. Isaiah called this person a Wonderful Counselor, Mighty God, Everlasting Father, and Prince of Peace. Whom do you think Isaiah's prophecy describes?** *(Jesus.)* **God promises us peace through Jesus.**

Story Follow-Up

M&P *Make copies of Reproducible Sheet E (TCK) and read through the directions for completing the activity. Have Leaflet 13 (LR) and pencils ready.*

Have the learners find "Prophecy Puzzle" on page 3 of their leaflets. Let them work in pairs or small groups to complete the crossword puzzle, referring to the Bible story on page 2 as needed. When everyone is finished, share the correct answers with the group. Then give each learner a copy of the reproducible sheet and tell them how to complete the activity.

Using a world map or globe, ask learners to choose a country they would like to learn about. What do the people of that country need most? How can we help?

Play a game of animal charades! Secretly assign each learner an animal. Have them take turns acting like their animal while the group guesses what they are portraying. Award small prizes (animal stickers or pencils) to each learner for "Best Growl," "Funniest Waddle," "Scariest Snarl," and so forth. Make sure everyone receives a prize.

Teacher Boost

A peaceful attitude sets the tone in your classroom. Remember, it can also help learners set a peaceful tone as they go about their week!

Witnesses in the World

Find out what world missions your congregation supports and learn what your class can do to help. Perhaps you can participate in a special collection of money, food, or clothing. Be sure to include the missions in your class prayers.

GREAT good byes

Play peaceful music as the learners leave today. Remind them to go in peace and serve the Lord!

Live the Story (25 minutes)

Ways to Witness

M&P *Have a variety of miscellaneous props available.*

How can we live in peace with others? (*Take turns playing on the computer; don't put anyone down, even "show-offs" or bullies; don't argue with my parents; help out at home, be nice to my sister/brother.*) Encourage the learners to discuss a variety of situations that call for peace. Then form small groups and invite each group to role-play a situation that involves conflict and how it can be resolved peacefully. Provide props for the learners to use as they wish. After the activity remind the learners that God helps us live in peace.

Kids Create

M&P *For Snakeskin Pencil Holder: Have clean soup cans with sharp edges taped, masking tape, brown shoe polish, and cleaning rags. For Fingerprint Cards: Have construction paper or card stock, inkpads, fine-tipped markers, and wet paper towels for cleanup. Make a sample of the project you choose.*

Snakeskin Pencil Holder: Show the learners a sample pencil holder, reminding them of the word adder in today's Bible story. Tell them that an adder is a kind of poisonous snake. Demonstrate how to rip small pieces of masking tape and then overlap them on a can. Completely cover the can with tape and then rub brown shoe polish over it, wiping the excess away with a rag so that the tape is lightly stained to look like snakeskin. Be sure to have the learners wash their hands after completing the project.

Fingerprint Animal Cards: Show the learners a sample card. Have them fold paper or cardstock to make a greeting card. Show them how to press their index finger or thumb on an inkpad and then onto their card, creating fingerprints. Let them use markers to add details, creating a variety of people and animals. Suggest they add scenery and other details to the card. When the cover is complete, have them write a peaceful message inside and make plans to give the card to a friend or family member.

Wrapping It Up

M&P *Have Leaflet 13 (LR), the Witness CD (TCK), and a CD player available.*

Play Track 13 on the Witness CD, 'The Peaceful Kingdom Comes," as the learners clean up and collect their leaflets, Bibles, and completed projects to take home. Point out the interesting activities on page 4 of the leaflet and encourage them to try the activities with their families. Talk about the Witness Words that appear on page 4. Help learners define the words and tell how they relate to today's Bible story. Then gather together for prayer: **Jesus, you bring peace to our lives. Thank you for this day and for the time we have shared. Help us to be peacemakers. Amen**

Mary, Faithful Woman of God

Session at a Glance	What You Need	What Learners Do
Ready for the Story (15 minutes)		
Welcome the Witnesses	• Poster E and Witness CD (TCK), CD player	• Review Big Ideas and discuss the Big Idea for Session 14.
Story Warm-Up	• Posters D, L and P (TCK), Activity Cards A and D (TCK), Faith Trait stickers (LR), the learners' copies of the Little Book of Faith Traits	• Review Faith Traits for Sessions 1-13, and learn the Faith Trait for this session: *patience*.
Story Fire-Up	• Messages sealed in envelopes	• Find and read special messages.
Explore the Story (20 minutes)		
Story Set-Up	• Poster B (TCK), Leaflet 14 and Session 14 stickers (LR), battery-operated camp lantern or candle and matches, pottery, whole grains, olives, dates or figs, flat bread, olive oil	• Discover what life was like for Bible times children. Taste some Bible times foods.
Storytelling	• Witness CD (TCK), Leaflet 14 (LR), Bibles, CD player	• Read the Bible story.
Story Follow-Up	• Leaflet 14 (LR), colored pencils or crayons, chalkboard and chalk or chart paper and marker	• Talk about how messages are shared.
Live the Story (25 minutes)		
Ways to Witness	• Poster K (TCK), Leaflet 14 (LR), pencils, crayons or markers	• Talk about ways they can share God's good news.
Kids Create	• Construction paper, craft foam, metallic chenille stems, curled paper, ribbon, scissors, glue • White posterboard, markers	• Make a Heart Angel Ornament or a "Joy to the World" Doorknob Wreath.
Wrapping It Up	• Witness CD (TCK), Leaflet 14 (LR), Christmas music CD, CD player	• Review the Witness Words and pray together.

Bible Text

Luke 1:26-56

Key Verse

For nothing will be impossible with God. Luke 1:37

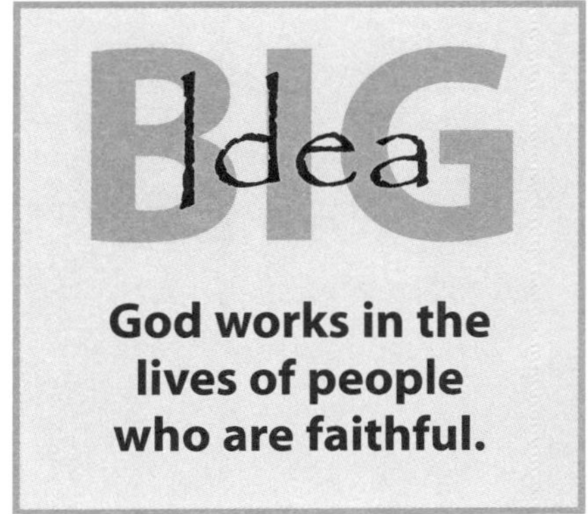

LR = Learner Resource
TCK = Teacher Class Kit
M&P = Materials and Preparation

Teacher Prayer

Thank you, God of hope, for Mary and other people like her who listen and respond to your call. Help me listen more carefully to your voice, especially as I teach your children. Amen

Question for Reflection

Who is a faithful person that you admire? What can you learn from that person?

Learner Goals

KNOW

the story of God's call to Mary and her faithful response

GROW

to understand what life was like for Bible times children

SHOW

patience and hope in their lives

FACTOID

In Mary and Joseph's context, their families would have negotiated and contracted their engagement not as a personal, but as a familial and social, joining.

Bible Background

What Factors Shaped This Story?

Only the Gospels of Matthew and Luke tell the story of Jesus' birth and infancy. Luke tells of both Jesus' and his cousin John's births—each remarkable. John's mother Elizabeth was presumed barren and was "getting on in years" (1:7); Mary was a virgin. In other women, as well as Elizabeth and Mary, Luke emphasizes Jesus' inclusion of women as important.

What Is This Story About?

"Do not be afraid" echoes again and again in this Gospel, including from Jesus himself. We shouldn't be surprised that God's ways might seem frightening since they are so different from our own. Mary's response is not fear but perplexity and sensible doubt. "How can this be?"(verse 34) she asks when the angel tells her she will have a child. She wants an explanation. When the explanation comes that it is God's will she is ready and willing to serve. Mary's devotion and faithfulness reflect a motif in the Gospel of Luke.

Through the centuries, Mary's song has been sung daily in the church. Those denominations and religious groups that sing daily vespers include her song "The Magnificat," after the word that begins her song in the Latin translation. Note how clearly the song proclaims God's power for justice. The proud, the powerful, and the rich are dispersed in favor of those who fear God, the lowly, and the hungry. When the angel tells Mary, "Nothing will be impossible with God" (verse 37), the angel speaks not only of her pregnancy, but of the justice God promises.

The work of the Holy Spirit is another important emphasis in Luke and Acts, also written by the author of Luke. In this story the Holy Spirit bears the power of God (verse 35) and fills Elizabeth with the knowledge not only of Mary's pregnancy but also of its significance.

Why Is This Story Important?

Mary's pregnancy and call to serve are examples of what Luke's Gospel proclaims—that Jesus' mission is universal. His vocation is the salvation of the whole world, including, perhaps especially, those whom the world puts on the margins, for example, young women such as Mary. By the power of the Holy Spirit, God will through Jesus fulfill God's promise of justice and peace.

Age-Level Connection

Third and fourth graders can learn from today's Bible story that Mary was faithful and listened to God's call, even though the angel's message may have seemed impossible. It is important for the learners to be reminded that God works through the lives of people of all ages. Trusting God is our most important expression of faith.

Ready for the Story (15 minutes)

Welcome the Witnesses

M&P *Display Poster E (Teacher Class Kit). Have music from the Witness CD (TCK) playing as the learners arrive.*

When everyone has arrived, ask the learners to tell the person sitting next to them one Big Idea they have learned. Then refer to Poster E as you read today's Big Idea together *(God works in the lives of people who are faithful).* **What does it mean to be a faithful person?** *(To trust God, to be trustworthy.)*

devotion, angel, patience

Story Warm-Up

M&P *Display Posters D and P (TCK). Have Poster L and Activity Card D (TCK) ready. Locate Activity Card A (TCK) and Faith Trait stickers (Learner Resource). Locate the learners' copies of the Little Book of Faith Traits (see Session 1 "Story Warm-Up").*

Ask a volunteer to distribute the Little Book of Faith Traits. Point to Poster D and have learners say today's Faith Trait together *(patience).* Have learners place today's Faith Trait sticker inside their booklets. Ask a volunteer to place today's marker from Activity Card A on Poster P. Note all the markers that have been placed on the poster. Ask learners to name the Faith Traits they represent. Praise them for learning about and living these Faith Traits in their daily lives. Collect and save the booklets for next time. Then place Poster L and the game cards from Activity Card D on a table or the floor. Gather the learners around the game and have fun reviewing the Faith Traits they have learned so far.

FACTOID

Angel is the Greek word for "messenger," though angels are often ascribed other roles. Gabriel is, along with Michael, the most prominent angel in biblical tradition.

Story Fire-Up

M&P *Before class, write a special message to each learner. For example, "*(Name)*, you are special to God and special to me!" Seal each message in an envelope and write the learner's name on the outside of the envelope. Hide the messages in your class area.*

Ask the learners to tell about times when they must be patient *(waiting for a friend or relative to visit, waiting for a special day).* **Sometimes it can be hard to wait patiently. At Christmas time, especially, it can be hard to wait!** Introduce the Witness Words for today. Define the word *devotion* by explaining that God calls us to devote ourselves to sharing the special message of God's love at Christmas time and always! Have the learners search for the hidden envelopes, finding the one addressed to them. Let them open their envelopes and read the special message from you!

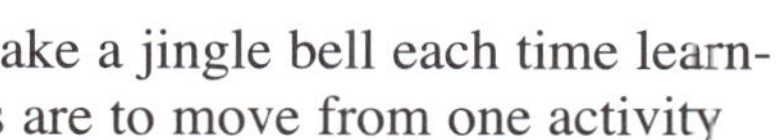

Transition Tip

Shake a jingle bell each time learners are to move from one activity to another.

Explore the Story (20 minutes)

Story Set-Up

M&P *Display Poster B (TCK). Have Leaflet 14 and Session 14 stickers (LR) available. Consider lighting your class area with a battery-operated camp lantern or candle. If lighting a candle, check your local fire codes and your congregation's fire policies regarding the use of open flames. Bring along items similar to those used in Bible times, such as pottery dishes or jugs, mortar and pestle, whole grains, olives, dates or figs, flat bread, and olive oil in a small bowl. Before serving any food, always check with caregivers for learners who have food allergies. Provide an alternative, if necessary.*

Spend a few minutes looking at Poster B and talking about the activities of Bible times children. Then show the learners the items you brought to class. If you have a mortar, pestle, and grain, let the learners take turns grinding the grain into flour. Invite the learners to taste flat bread dipped in olive oil. Then gather together and distribute the leaflets and stickers. Find "Life in Bible Times" on page 1 and ask volunteers to read the captions that accompany the pictures. Give learners time to add their stickers to the page. **How are your household chores the same or different from Mary's?** *(Accept all answers.)*

Provide Bible times costumes and props for the learners to use in dramatizing some of the Bible stories you have explored this term.

Storytelling

M&P *Have the Witness CD (TCK), Leaflet 14 (LR), pencils, and Bibles available. Also have a CD player available.*

Have the learners turn to page 2 in their leaflets. Ask a volunteer to read the Bible Text, Big Idea, and Key Verse aloud. Help learners find Luke 1:26-56 in their Bibles and take turns reading the story aloud. Then let partners review the story by completing the activity on page 2 of the leaflet. *(Answers in order: Gabriel, Nazareth, Galilee, Joseph, Lord, with, angel, greeting, afraid, baby, son, Jesus, Son, Holy Spirit, holy, nothing, impossible, servant, cousin, Elizabeth, baby, Blessed, Son, praised, love, care.)* When everyone is ready, read the story together from the leaflet. **Even though Mary was surprised by the angel's message, she trusted God. God works in the lives of people who are faithful.** Play "I Bring You Good News," Track 14 on the Witness CD. Invite the learners to listen to the song, then play it again and sing along!

Set chairs in a tic-tac-toe pattern in an open area. Form two teams. Have learners answer Bible story review questions from this session and previous sessions. If a learner answers correctly, he or she sits on one of the chairs. The first team to get three in a row wins!

Story Follow-Up

M&P *Have Leaflet 14 (LR), colored pencils or crayons, chalkboard and chalk or chart paper and marker available.*

Write "Angel" on the chalkboard or chart paper. **The angel shared an important message with Mary. Who or what shares messages with us today?** As the learners share ideas, write them on the chalkboard or chart paper. Then have everyone find "Messengers" on page 3 of their leaflets. Provide colored pencils or crayons for completing the activity. Then ask the learners to compare the messengers they revealed on page 3 with the list created earlier. Emphasize that God gives us many ways to share messages and the greatest message of all to share: Jesus!

Live the Story (25 minutes)

Ways to Witness

M&P *Display Poster K (TCK). Have Leaflet 14 (LR), pencils, crayons or markers available.*

Point to Samuel and Gideon on Poster K. **What do you remember about Samuel and Gideon?** *(God called Samuel's name, telling him to share an important message with Eli; God called Gideon to help the Israelites.)* Then point to Mary and note that God called her to be the mother of Jesus. **Who else is mentioned on this poster?** *(You!)* **God calls you to share the good news!** Have learners find "Sharing the Good News" on page 3 of their leaflets. Read the introduction and then talk about ways we can tell others about Jesus. *(E-mail Bible verses to a friend, perform in a Christmas program, sing praises to God.)* Give the learners time to write about or draw their ideas in the space provided on page 3.

Kids Create

M&P *For Heart Angel Ornament: For each learner cut one large heart, two medium hearts, one small heart, and one small circle from construction paper or craft foam (see diagram). Provide metallic chenille stems, curled paper or ribbon, additional strands of ribbon, scissors, and glue. For "Joy to the World" Doorknob Wreath: Have white poster board cut into 8" (20 cm) circles, assorted colors of construction paper, adult scissors, pencils, markers, and glue. Make a sample of the project you choose.*

Heart Angel Ornament: Show the learners a sample ornament and say that the angel is a reminder that Mary was called by God. Demonstrate how to glue medium hearts to the large heart for wings. Add a circle for the angel's head, curled paper for hair, and the small heart for the angel's folded hands. Have learners cut and bend chenille stems into circles to glue to the top of their angel's head for a halo. Attach a loop of ribbon to the back of the angel for hanging.

"Joy to the World" Doorknob Wreath: Show learners a sample wreath. Give a poster board circle to each learner and have each one cut a circle from its center, creating a wreath. Talk about symbols they might include on their wreaths, such as the earth, stars, a manger, or stable. Suggest they also add peaceful animals from the Isaiah 11:1-9 text discussed during Session 13. Give them time to color their wreaths and then cut shapes from construction paper, gluing them on.

Wrapping It Up

M&P *Have Track 14 of the Witness CD (TCK) or Christmas music playing as you end today's session. Have Leaflet 14 (LR) available.*

Have the learners collect their leaflets, Bibles, and completed projects. Look at page 4 of the leaflet and point out the fun activities they can try with their families. Talk about the Witness Words that appear on that page. Help them define the words and then tell how they relate to today's Bible story. Close with prayer: **Thank you, God, for having such great plans—plans that we could never begin to think of! Thank you especially for loving us so much that you had the plan to send Jesus to be our Savior! Amen**

Teacher Boost

Your faithfulness to God's call is evident in the time you spend preparing and presenting each session. Your dedication is appreciated by your learners, their caregivers, and leaders involved in your Sunday school program.

Witnesses in the World

Work with the director of a local homeless shelter, and with the learners' caregivers, to purchase warm socks that can be stuffed with packaged chewing gum, soap, toothpaste, candy, playing cards, or other small items. If possible deliver the "Christmas stockings" to the shelter as a class.

Play Christmas music as the learners leave and have them look into a mirror as a reminder that God's work is reflected in their lives!

Jesus Is Born!

Bible Text

Luke 2:1-20

Key Verse

And she gave birth to her firstborn son and wrapped him in bands of cloth, and laid him in a manger, because there was no place for them in the inn. Luke 2:7

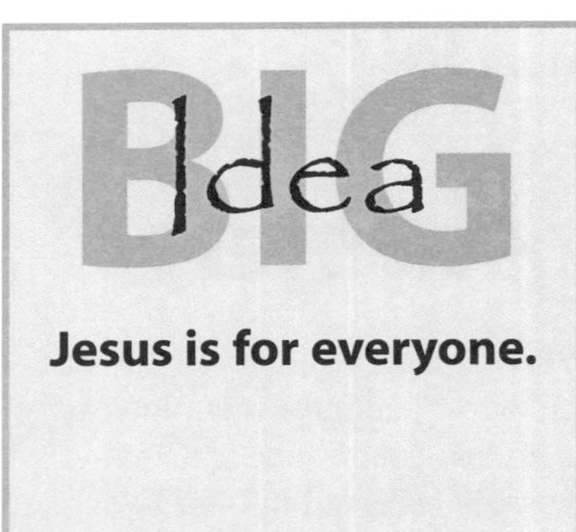

LR = Learner Resource
TCK = Teacher Class Kit
M&P = Materials and Preparation

Session at a Glance	What You Need	What Learners Do
Ready for the Story (15 minutes)		
Welcome the Witnesses	• Poster E and Witness CD (TCK), CD player	• Review Big Ideas from Sessions 1-14 and learn the Big Idea for Session 15.
Story Warm-Up	• Posters D, L and P (TCK), Activity Cards A and D (TCK), Faith Trait stickers (LR), the learners' copies of the Little Book of Faith Traits	• Learn today's Faith Trait, *joy*, and play a game to review all the semester's Faith Traits.
Story Fire-Up	• Poster O (TCK), Leaflet 15 (LR), holiday items or nativity figures, reusable adhesive putty or thumbtacks	• Search for signs and symbols of Christmas.
Explore the Story (20 minutes)		
Story Set-Up	• A crèche or nativity figures	• Discuss the Witness Words.
Storytelling	• Leaflet 15 (LR), Bibles, markers or crayons, Christmas music CD, CD player	• Read the Bible story.
Story Follow-Up	• Leaflet 15 (LR)	• Unscramble a word puzzle.
Live the Story (25 minutes)		
Ways to Witness	• Reproducible Sheet F (TCK), fine-tipped markers, Christmas stickers, chalkboard and chalk or chart paper and marker	• Make coupons to give as gifts.
Kids Create	• Craft sticks, toothpicks, wooden spoons, cardboard, fabric scraps, craft glue, scissors, raffia • Felt, fabric scraps, fabric glue, stencils, yarn, dowels	• Make a Nativity Scene or "Jesus is for Everyone!" Flag.
Wrapping It Up	• Witness CD (TCK), Leaflet 15 (LR), or Christmas music CD, CD player, Little Book of Faith Traits	• Review the Witness Words and pray an ABC prayer.

Bible Background

What Factors Shaped This Story?

The Roman Emperor Augustus ruled from 27 B.C.E. to 14 C.E. At the time of Jesus' birth, Palestine had been under Roman occupation for about 100 years. The Roman government exploited the people, who hoped for a leader who would bring justice and peace. "The world" referred to in verse 1 is the Roman empire. The Gospel writer Luke is both historian and preacher. Luke is intent on locating the story of salvation amidst specific times, places, and events of history. Salvation is God at work in history; history is the realm of God's activity.

What Is This Story About?

In a corner of a colony of Roman empire comes the birth of a child. While emperor and military governor exercise power, an engaged couple travel, despite her pregnancy, to obey the emperor's decree. While world events transpire, God's messengers visit shepherds in their fields. The birth of the Savior comes in a specific historical time and place to turn the world upside down. The focus is on angels rather than on an emperor, on God's messengers rather than on imperial decree, on a newborn child rather than on obedience to the colonial power, on a manger in a stable in a small town rather than on a palace or grand house in a capital city. In the Roman world, the emperor was understood to be God's designated leader. Indeed, the emperor was himself considered divine. For Luke, the new child whose birth proclaims peace is God's chosen leader, "the Messiah" or *Christ*, which means "anointed."

Why Is This Story Important?

The center of world events is not necessarily Rome or Jerusalem or any world capital or other seat of worldly power. The center of world events is where God is bringing peace and salvation for all people. God's actions are not remote. Heaven and earth are not far from one another. Angels from heaven speak to shepherds in the fields. The Messiah is a human child.

Age-Level Connection

As you tell the story of Jesus' birth, enjoy your group's excitement and anticipation of the greatest gift we have ever received—God's gift of a Savior! Most third and fourth graders will be eager to find ways to share the good news and their gifts with others, so they will likely enjoy the activities in this session.

Teacher Prayer

Savior of the world, thank you for entering our lives each day, and for being the light in the darkness that we so desperately need. Thank you most of all for the privilege of spending time with these children. Amen

Question for Reflection

How will you keep the birth of the Christ child at the center of your Christmas celebration this year?

Learner Goals

KNOW
the story of Jesus' birth

GROW
in understanding that God loves them and all people

SHOW
joy in celebrating the birth of our Savior

FACTOID

The "registration" that took Mary and Joseph to Bethlehem was a census required for purposes of taxation and conscription into military service.

Ready for the Story (15 minutes)

Welcome the Witnesses

M&P *Display Poster E (Teacher Class Kit). Have "Jesus Is Born! Let's Celebrate!" (Track 15) on the Witness CD (TCK) playing as the learners arrive.*

Use Poster E to review all the Big Ideas you have learned this semester. Then introduce today's Big Idea *(Jesus is for everyone)*. Talk about the excitement that surrounds Christmas. Let the learners share stories that reflect their anticipation. Then help them return their focus to the birth of Jesus as the center of the Christmas celebration.

Story Warm-Up

M&P *Display Posters D and P (TCK). Have Poster L and Activity Cards A and D (TCK) ready. Locate Faith Trait stickers (LR) and the learners' copies of the Little Book of Faith Traits (see Session 1 "Story Warm-Up").*

Ask a volunteer to distribute the Little Book of Faith Traits and Faith Trait stickers. Point to today's Faith Trait on Poster D and invite the learners to say it together *(joy)*. Have them place today's sticker on its corresponding page in their booklets. Then ask a learner to place the marker from Activity Card A on Poster P. Take time to review all the Faith Trait words and symbols that appear on the poster. **Today's Faith Trait, *joy*, sums up how we feel when we reflect all of these Faith Traits in our lives.** Collect the Little Book of Faith Traits and save them until the end of the session. Next, place Poster L and the game cards from Activity Card D on a table or the floor. Gather the learners to play this game one last time, reviewing all the Faith Traits they have learned.

Story Fire-Up

M&P *Locate Poster O (TCK) and Leaflet 15 (LR). Before class, hide several holiday items in the class area, such as a Christmas book, cookie cutter, star ornament, and toy snowman, or hide the figures from a nativity set. Have reusable adhesive putty or thumbtacks available.*

I need your help to solve a mystery! I brought some special Christmas items with me today, but they have disappeared! Can you help me find them? Give the learners time to find the hidden items, arranging them at the center of your meeting area. Then display Poster O on a wall or bulletin board. Give the learners time to find some of the hidden objects on the poster. Is this harder or easier than looking for the real things in the classroom? Then distribute the leaflets and have partners work together to complete "Christmas Find" on page 1.

emperor, decree, census, manger

FACTOID

Bethlehem, six miles (9.6 kilometers) south of Jerusalem, is King David's birthplace. Jesus' birth fulfills Micah's prophecy (Micah 5:2-4) that a new king will come from there.

Transition Tip

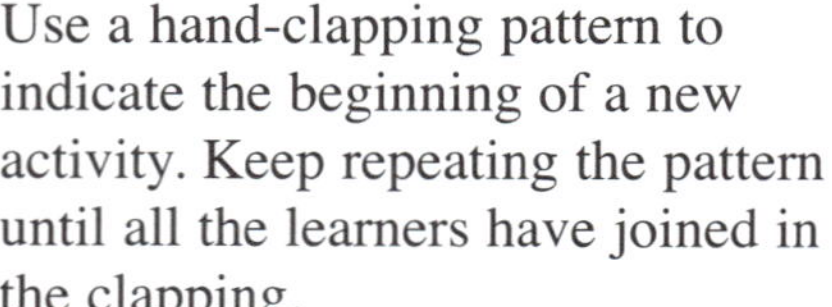

Use a hand-clapping pattern to indicate the beginning of a new activity. Keep repeating the pattern until all the learners have joined in the clapping.

Explore the Story (20 minutes)

Story Set-Up

M&P *Locate a crèche or figures from a nativity scene.*
Show the learners the crèche or nativity figures you have brought to class. Have them identify various characters and objects including the holy family, shepherds, angels, animals, stable, and manger. Talk with the learners about the poor conditions at the time of the story. Share today's Witness Words and talk about their meaning: *emperor* (a ruler); *decree* (an order given by the emperor); *census* (a record of all the people living in a particular area or country); *manger* (an animal feeding trough). Tell learners that governments still take censuses today, although people usually do not have to travel from their homes in order to be counted. But in Bible times, Mary and Joseph were ordered to travel to Joseph's hometown, Bethlehem, along with many other people, to be counted. With so many people visiting the small town of Bethlehem, there was no place for Mary and Joseph to stay, except in a stable.

Talk about gifts the learners hope to receive, and plan to give, this Christmas. Emphasize how gift giving relates to the gift of Jesus, and to the Wise Men's gifts.

Storytelling

M&P *Have Leaflet 15 (LR), Bibles, pencils, and markers or crayons available. Locate a Christmas music CD and CD player.*
Have the learners turn to page 2 in their leaflets. Ask a volunteer to read the Bible Text, Big Idea, and Key Verse aloud. Help the learners find Luke 2:1-20 in their Bibles and take turns reading the story aloud. Afterward, ask the learners to complete the story scenes on page 2 of their leaflets. Play Christmas music while the learners work on the activity. Encourage them to tell about their favorite part of the Christmas story. **Why is that your favorite part? How does it remind you of God's love?** When the learners complete page 2, ask them to share their drawings with the class.

More Movement

Play lively music from a Christmas CD and invite the learners to jingle bells and dance to their own "jingle bell hop!"

Story Follow-Up

M&P *Have Leaflet 15 (LR) and pencils available.*
Ask the learners to name some things they do to get ready for Christmas *(wrap gifts, decorate, bake cookies)*. Then have them find "Christmas is Coming!" on page 3 of their leaflets. Let partners work together to unscramble the phrases and draw pictures. *(Answers: shop for gifts, send cards, bake cookies, sing at church.)* Then have learners create their own Christmas phrases for their partners to unscramble. **There are many things we can do to get ready for Christmas. But most importantly, we can thank God for the gift of a Savior. Jesus is for everyone.**

Teacher Boost

As you end this session, find satisfaction in knowing that you and your group have learned from each other, and have had the opportunity to learn more about God's great love.

Witnesses in the World

If your class collected Christmas stocking items for people living in homeless shelters (see Session 14 Witnesses in the World), prepare the stockings today. Take time to write joyful messages to include with each gift.

Go Global!

Read the Go Global! activity on Reproducible Sheets S and T (TCK). See page 3.

Play Christmas music as the learners leave and give each of them a small gift. Tell them how much you have enjoyed your time together this semester.

Live the Story (25 minutes)

Ways to Witness

M&P *Make copies of Reproducible Sheet F (TCK). Each learner should receive several coupons from this sheet. Have fine-tipped markers, Christmas stickers, a chalkboard and chalk or chart paper and marker available.*

The best gifts are those that are given from the heart, so making "helper coupons" to give as gifts is a wonderful way to let learners discover that the gift of themselves is the best gift of all. Distribute coupons to the learners and help them think of gifts they could give to others. For example, they could walk or feed the dog, help with the dishes, or prepare a simple meal. Have them write their ideas on the coupons. If learners need help spelling certain words, write them on a chalkboard or chart paper for copying. Let learners decorate their coupons with stickers and drawings. Make sure they sign each one!

Kids Create

M&P *For Nativity Scene: Provide narrow and wide craft sticks, toothpicks, wooden ice cream spoons, cardboard, fabric scraps, craft glue, scissors, and raffia (available at craft stores). For "Jesus Is for Everyone!" Flag: Have one 9" x 12" (23 cm x 30 cm) piece of felt per learner, assorted felt and fabric scraps, fabric glue, pencils or pens, stencils, scissors, yarn, and one 12" (30 cm) dowel per learner. Make a sample of the project you choose.*

Nativity Scene: Show the learners a sample Nativity Scene. Help the learners arrange and glue the craft sticks to create a floor, walls, and stable roof. Provide toothpicks and cardboard for creating a manger and star. Place raffia in the manger for straw. Use wooden spoons, fabric scraps, and fine-tipped markers to create the nativity characters. Encourage everyone to experiment and have fun!

"Jesus Is for Everyone!" Flag: Show the learners a sample flag. Give each learner a piece of felt for the background of the flag. Have them draw and cut out letters and shapes from felt and fabric scraps using stencils, if they wish. Have them arrange everything on their flag before gluing. Show the learners how to fold and glue the top edge of their flag, creating a casing. When dry, slide a dowel through the casing and tie on yarn for hanging.

Wrapping It Up

M&P *Play Track 16 of the Witness CD (TCK) or other Christmas music. Have Leaflet 15 (LR) and the learners' copies of the Little Book of Faith Traits available.*

Have the learners collect their leaflets, Bibles, and completed projects. Distribute their Little Book of Faith Traits to take home. Encourage them to share the booklets and the activities on page 4 of their leaflets with their families. Review today's Witness Words on page 4 and then ask the learners to join you in an ABC Prayer. Begin the prayer by thanking God for your time together this semester, and for the good news that Jesus is for everyone. Then invite learners to take turns naming things they are thankful for that begin with each letter of the alphabet (*"Thank you, God, for **a**pples.... for **b**rothers.... for **c**aring teachers..." and so forth*). Conclude the prayer with a big "Amen!"

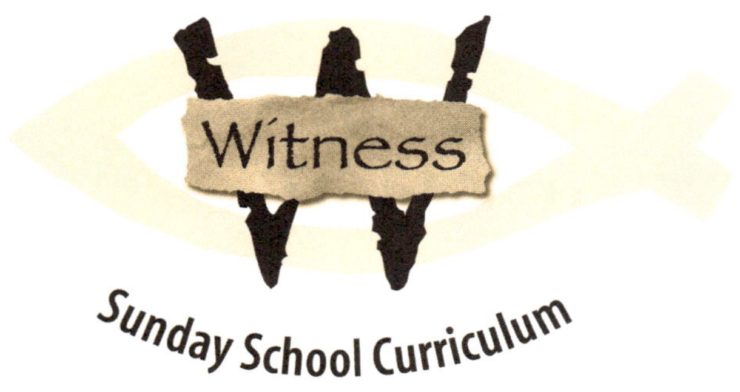

Bonus Sessions

What Are Bonus Sessions?

The five Bonus sessions during each semester of Witness offer theme-based learning opportunities in a shorter, particularly flexible format. Bonus sessions provide additional content for Sunday school programs that need more than 15 sessions per semester. They can also be used when teachers want experiential learning with a different pace.

What Is the Content of Bonus Sessions?

Bonus sessions offer the same set of categories represented by different Bible stories in each semester. In the **Jesus' Teachings** category, learners take a look at one or more of Jesus' teachings. Learners make **Old Testament/New Testament Connections** when they compare and contrast related Old and New Testament texts. Each semester, learners can take a **Field Trip** to explore a space outside of the classroom. A **Seasonal Preparations** session is offered each semester to provide an additional session on Advent (Semester 1) or Lent (Semester 2). Bonus sessions in the **Worship** category provide a time for learners to investigate faith practices and worship styles.

When Should I Use Bonus Sessions?

Bonus sessions can be plugged into the schedule at any time. If you have one, the Sunday school coordinator should coordinate group plans, especially related to Seasonal Preparations. Ask your Sunday school planner if Bonus sessions across age and grade levels will be planned for the same day, or if you have flexibility in scheduling them. If you are doing your own planning, browse through the Bonus sessions to see which ones you'd like to use and when.

What Are the Parts of a Bonus Session?

The first page of each Bonus session gets teachers and kids ready to learn. Pre-class preparation helps for the teacher, and one or more Ready for the Story activities for kids launch the Bible story investigations. The second page provides Explore the Story and Live the Story options for digging into the Bible story and making life applications. Some of the same sidebar headings from Core sessions are included in Bonus sessions.

What Do Learners Use during Bonus Sessions?

The learner resource for the Bonus sessions has two parts, neither of which is part of the Core learner resource. Each Bonus session has one reproducible page printed in the teacher guide and one reproducible sheet found in the teacher class kit. Be sure to make arrangements for timely and efficient photocopying of the appropriate pages and sheets for your group.

Christian Connections

Bible Text

John 15:1-17

Key Verse

[Jesus said], "I am the vine, you are the branches. Those who abide in me and I in them bear much fruit, because apart from me you can do nothing." John 15:5

We are connected to God and each other.

M&P

READY FOR THE STORY

Copies of Reproducible Page A (page 00 in Teacher Guide), Bibles, nametags, colored pencils or markers, grape snacks (grape juice, grapes, raisins, and fruit snacks). Before serving any food, always check with caregivers for learners who have food allergies. Provide an alternative, if necessary.

Bible Background

John 14–17 is Jesus' farewell speech. Jesus leaves a legacy and gives instruction for life after his death. Jesus talks about our relationship to him and to God the Father, to one another, and to the world. Then he prays for himself, his immediate disciples, and the whole church.

The vine and branches are one image of how we as believers are together in Christ. Visualize a vine and its branches. See how the vine and the branches together make the plant. Abiding in Christ the vine we abide in relationship with one another. When Jesus says that "apart from me you can do nothing" (verse 5), he is also talking about our relationships to one another. A branch cut off from the vine and apart from other branches cannot survive. The vine is an image also for Jesus' words (verses 3, 7) and love (verses 9-10), which also bear and sustain us together. Abiding in Jesus' words and God's love we live, thrive, and bear fruit.

As branches are sustained on a vine, we are sustained in Christ. As branches are one plant sprouted from and joined on a vine, in Christ we are born and joined together. Christ is love, nurtures and sustains us with love, and bequeaths love to us for loving one another. As Christ the vine sustains us in love, so we sustain one another. Our lives are joyful (verse 11) when we live mindful of this reality.

Ready for the Story (10 minutes)

Greet learners and distribute nametags, Bibles, Reproducible Page A, and markers or pencils. Learners can decorate their nametags with grapes and work on the puzzles. When all learners arrive, share grape snacks as you talk about grapes. **Vineyards and grapes are mentioned many times in the New Testament. Jesus' first miracle was turning water into fine wine at a friend's wedding.** Remind learners that grapes are used to make the wine and juice for communion. Explain how the wine from vineyards provided people with a safe beverage during a time when water was often unsafe to drink. **During the Last Supper with his disciples, Jesus referred to the wine as his blood, and the bread as his body.** Ask how many learners take Communion or are preparing for first communion.

Explore the Story (25 minutes)

Ask a volunteer to read John 15:1-17. Read the passage again, stopping after verses about branches, vines, and fruit. Talk about Jesus' comparisons to the environment that describe his relationship with believers. Explain why pruning is necessary. Talk about what it means to bear fruit. Read the passage a third time without interruptions.

Show the grapevine wreath to learners. Point out the interconnectedness of vines and branches. Ask a learner to try removing just one vine from the wreath. Explain that Jesus' description of the vineyard helps us understand how we are connected to Jesus and each other. **We can trust Jesus to be our vine. Others who believe in Jesus are like the branches on this wreath—it's hard to separate us! Today's Faith Trait is cooperation. When we cooperate with others who believe in Jesus, we can bear good fruit together.** Share a story from your own life about how you have felt connected to other Christians, and how cooperation helped you bear good fruit.

Go outside to show learners the connectedness between branches, trunks, and vines. Point out dead twigs, leaves, and branches. Explain how removing these parts keeps the plants healthy. Use gardening tools to prune.

M&P

EXPLORE THE STORY
Bibles, grapevine wreath, gardening tools

LIVE THE STORY
Copies of Reproducible Sheet N (TCK), picture of a vineyard, construction paper (green, brown, and purple), long sheet of butcher paper, glue sticks, grapes, spoons, juicer

Live the Story (25 minutes)

Prepare the necessary materials for two or three activities. Finish with the Closing Prayer, and distribute copies of Reproducible Sheet N.

Grapevine Mural

Show a picture of a vineyard. Distribute construction paper. Learners can tear brown sheets into long strips, green sheets into leaf shapes, and purple sheets into grape shapes. On a long sheet of butcher paper, learners can glue the pieces to show a long vine, branches from the vine, and grape clusters and leaves at the end of branches. Emphasize cooperation as they make the mural.

Grape Relay

Split learners into two lined-up teams and give each learner a spoon. Place 10 grapes in the front of each line and empty cups at the end. Team members must pass one grape at a time from spoon to spoon without dropping the grape. If a grape falls, it must go back to the beginning of the line and be passed again. The winning team is the one that gets all the grapes in the cup first. Have extra grapes handy in case some are squashed. Emphasize cooperation as they play the relay.

Tasty Juice

Help learners juice bunches of grapes. Learners can wash grapes, pull them off the stems, and place them in the juicer compartment. Emphasize cooperation as they prepare the juice. Since fresh juice is very strong, each learner only needs a small serving. Let learners know that this is what grape juice tasted like during Bible times.

DeVINE Rap

Show learners "DeVINE Rap" on Reproducible Page A. Ask for volunteers to practice and perform the rap. Teach the refrain to all learners.

Closing Prayer

Dear Jesus, thank you for loving and supporting us. Help us stay connected to you and to each other. Amen

Learner Goals

KNOW
the vineyard comparison Jesus used

GROW
in understanding their connectedness to other Christians

SHOW
cooperation with others

Teacher Prayer

Dear God, our Gardener, thank you for your wonderful creation and for Jesus, our vine. Help us to cling to Jesus and stay connected to others so that we may do your will and bear your fruit. Amen

Question for Reflection

What parts of your life need pruning and what parts are bearing good fruit?

Bread of Life

Bible Text

John 6:22-35; Exodus 16:1-16

Key Verse

In the morning you shall have your fill of bread; then you shall know that I am the LORD your God. Exodus 16:12

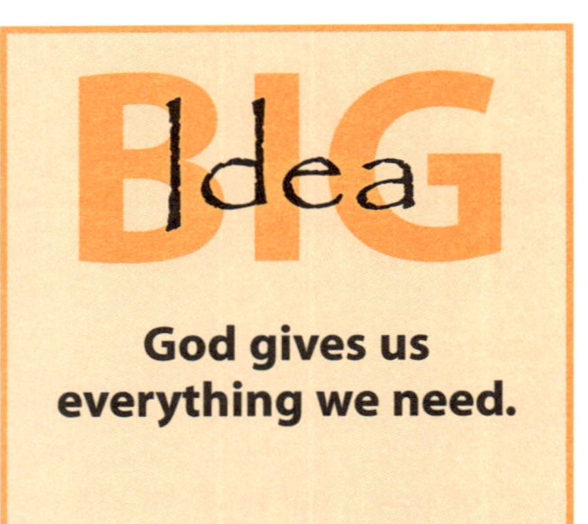

M&P

READY FOR THE STORY

Napkins, variety of leavened and unleavened bread, crackers, and wafers (many grocery stores carry different types in the ethnic food section). Before serving any food, always check with caregivers for learners who have food allergies. Provide an alternative, if necessary.

Bible Background

The people crossing the sea (John 6:22-24) recall the ancient people's crossing the sea to freedom (Exodus 14:21-24). In the desert, God provided food: manna or bread from heaven, and water. God provided enough for everyone—not too much or too little. Earlier in John 6, Jesus fed thousands of people, making enough from one boy's five barley loaves and two fish.

People responded to Jesus being able to feed so many people. Anyone who has the resources to feed a hungry multitude can command an audience. In fact, the crowd sought to make Jesus king (John 6:15), not only that his power would provide food for them but also that his power might liberate them from Roman occupation as Moses had liberated the people from Egyptian slavery. People expected these things of the promised Messiah.

Jesus points beyond the food that fills bellies to the food that endures and sustains life. Yet that divine food, he says, "comes down from heaven and gives life to the world" (John 6:33). Heaven and earth are joined in that food. God's work and human work are joined, and God's work is in believers' believing and following Jesus.

Jesus stands in the traditions of the people, continues those traditions, and does something new. He is both like Moses and different from Moses. He not only gives bread but also is himself bread, not earthly food, but relationship with Jesus who was sent from heaven to the world. As God provided food in the wilderness for the people, God provides food for us in our need. God feeds and nourishes not only our bodies but our whole selves. In Jesus, God gives us the Bread of life.

Ready for the Story (10 minutes)

Before the session, purchase bread products like loaves, crackers, and wafers. If several groups plan this Bonus session on the same Sunday, share different breads with other groups. As learners arrive, invite them to sample the breads. Talk about the different textures and flavors. Ask about breads served at home and favorite types. **People around the world grind a variety of flours and prepare many kinds of bread. Old Testament people made and ate bread. In many places around the world with hungry people, we send grain so they can make and eat bread.**

Explore the Story (25 minutes)

Distribute Bibles and Reproducible Page B. Provide background for today's story by reviewing how God called Moses to lead the Israelites out of Egyptian slavery into a land of their own. Recall details about the Red Sea story. **Today we will hear about Moses and the Israelites receiving food from the sky after the**

Israelites complained about not having enough food. What do you complain about sometimes? *(Accept learner responses.)* **This story shows that God provides what we need.** Help learners find Exodus 16:1-16. Volunteers can read parts of the Lord, Moses, Aaron, and the narrator. All learners can read the Israelites's part. Then guide learners through "Whiny Travelers" on Reproducible Page B.

Guide learners to find John 6:22-35. **Jesus turned a boy's lunch into enough food to feed thousands of people. Some of these people found him the next day.** Ask for volunteers to read the parts of Jesus, the narrator, and the crowd. Point out verses 31-32 that refer to the story of the Israelites receiving manna. **In the New Testament, people talked about what happened during the times of Moses and other people in the Old Testament. Jesus knew these stories because he had studied these scriptures.**

Live the Story (25 minutes)

Prepare the necessary materials for two or three activities. Finish the session with the Closing Prayer, and distribute copies of Reproducible Sheet O.

Food for All

Before the session, explore the Bread for the World website (www.bread.org). **These Bible stories show us that God provided food when the people were hungry and that Jesus is the Bread of life we all need for eternal life. In some places, people do not have enough to eat each day. God calls us to share with others. Let's think about how we could help people who are hungry.** Share your findings from the website.

A Meal with Jesus

Let's think about what we would do if Jesus actually visited us today. Guide learners through "Bread of Life Banquet" on Reproducible Page B. Help them make plans for a visit from Jesus.

Making Manna

Show the ingredients for the manna. **The Bible tells us that manna tasted like honey and the Israelites ground it into flour to make pancakes.** Combine equal parts of smooth peanut butter, honey, oatmeal, and dry milk. Give learners turns to stir. Distribute two sheets of waxed paper to each learner, give each learner a piece, and show them how to roll it into thin pancakes. Eat and enjoy!

Bread of Life Recipes

Distribute the recipe or index cards. Show learners how to write recipes for "Bread from Heaven," "Life with Jesus," or other creative titles. Include servings, pinches, and dashes of things like trust, generosity, and studying the Bible. Learners can give the cards to family or friends.

Closing Prayer

Dear God, thank you for giving us enough to eat each day. Thank you for giving us Jesus, our Bread of life. Amen

M&P

EXPLORE THE STORY

Copies of Reproducible Page B (page 00 in Teacher Guide), Bibles, a world map or globe

LIVE THE STORY

Copies of Reproducible Sheet O (TCK), recipe cards or index cards, pens or pencils, mixing bowls, mixing spoons, waxed paper, rolling pins, 1-cup measuring cup, smooth peanut butter, honey, dry oatmeal, dry milk or unsweetened soy milk powder

Learner Goals

KNOW

God provides daily bread

GROW

in understanding how Jesus is the Bread of life

SHOW

concern for people who are hungry

Teacher Prayer

Dear God, we trust you to provide us with all we need—food, clothing, shelter, and your nourishing love. Thank you for the gift of your own son, Jesus. Amen

Question for Reflection

When do you complain about what God has provided?

The Sacrament of Baptism

Bible Text

Romans 6:1-11; Acts 2:37-42

Key Verse

Peter said to them, "Repent, and be baptized every one of you in the name of Jesus Christ so that your sins may be forgiven; and you will receive the gift of the Holy Spirit." Acts 2:38

Baptism welcomes us into God's family.

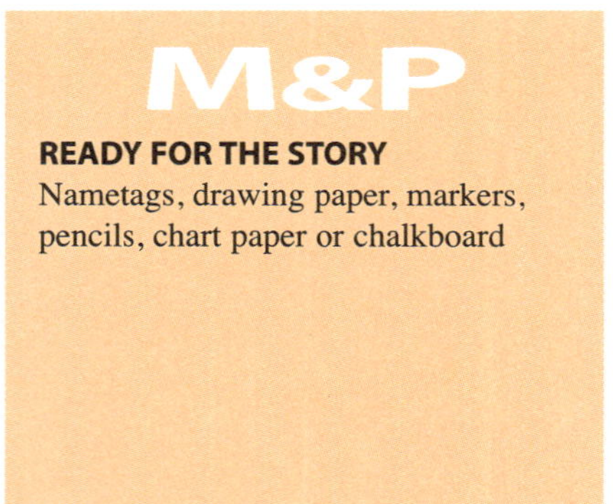

READY FOR THE STORY
Nametags, drawing paper, markers, pencils, chart paper or chalkboard

Bible Background

Baptism is the rite of initiation into the Christian community. Various religions include rites of purification and initiation, including washing with water. As a Christian sacrament, Holy Baptism is a means of God's grace with an outward sign (water) and God's promise of our salvation as children of God. Christians today don't always agree about what age baptism is appropriate; what, if anything, is required; and the physical method of baptizing.

Paul taught that God's salvation was for all who believe. Believers receive salvation in Christ by being united with Christ in Holy Baptism. This means being united not only with his life, but also with his death and new life. Believers are free from sin and death. This doesn't mean that believers no longer sin or die. It means that sin and death no longer exercise power over believers who are free to live new lives and not to sin.

Romans and Acts emphasize changing one's mind and life in response to belief in Jesus Christ. Baptism conveys the forgiveness of sins and the gift of the Holy Spirit who empowers believers for life in Christian community. Being members of the Christian community and followers of Jesus Christ make a difference in one's life. Believers' lives are devoted to the "apostles' teaching and fellowship, to the breaking of bread and the prayers" (Acts 2:42).

Scripture teaches us the practice of baptism but witnesses a variety of teaching and practice regarding Holy Baptism. At the center of Holy Baptism is a life-transforming relationship with God in Christ Jesus: we are united with Jesus and freed from sin and death. Freed and forgiven, we can live our lives devoted to God and to one another.

Ready for the Story (10 minutes)

Write *shell, candle, cross, dove, fish,* and *candle* on chart paper or the chalkboard. Ask learners to draw a few of these objects on their nametags. **A symbol stands for, or reminds us of, something important. Colors can be symbols. The color yellow on road signs is a symbol to be careful. Green is a symbol for new life. Shapes and objects are also symbols. A circle is a symbol of God's love because it never ends, just like God's love for us never ends.** Encourage learners to think of other symbols. **In the church, many symbols help us remember important things.** Point to the nametags. **You drew some symbols of baptism. We'll learn more about them on a baptism field trip.**

Explore the Story (20 minutes)

If possible, invite your pastor to this field trip. Guide learners to the worship space and sit or stand around the baptismal font. Bring Bibles and baptismal symbols to the font. **Today we will read about baptism in the Bible.**

Ask a learner to read Mark 1:9-11. Ask learners to describe what the baptism of Jesus must have looked like to those people watching on the shores of the Jordan. Hold up the dove and candle. **A dove is a symbol of the Holy Spirit that God sent after Jesus was baptized. Another symbol of the Holy Spirit is fire, like the candle that is usually lit when a person is baptized.**

Ask a volunteer to read Acts 2:37-42. Talk about what it must have looked like when 3,000 people were being baptized. Hold up the bowl of water and the shell. **In this story, we learn that about 3,000 people were baptized that day. This story shows us that water is a symbol for being washed clean of sins. Another symbol of baptism is a shell because it reminds us of water.**

Ask a volunteer to read Romans 6:1-11. Talk about the death that Paul writes about, explaining how it means that we die to sin and start a new life. Hold up the cross. **These verses tell us that baptism connects us to Jesus. The cross can be a symbol of baptism because it reminds us that Jesus died for us so that we can have new life! Another symbol we may see during baptism is a fish, because a fish was a symbol of Jesus for the first Christians.**

M&P

EXPLORE THE STORY
Bibles, bowl of water, scalloped shell, fish, small jar of oil, white candle, cross, white baptismal gown, and other baptismal symbols or gifts used in your church

LIVE THE STORY
Copies of Reproducible Page C (page 00 in Teacher Guide) and Reproducible Sheet P (TCK), Bibles, hymnals, index cards, pencils or pens, scissors, construction paper, stapler or string

Live the Story (30 minutes)

Prepare the necessary materials for each activity. Finish the session with the Closing Prayer, and distribute copies of Reproducible Sheet P.

Symbol Search

Take learners on a baptism field trip in your worship space to look for baptismal symbols in the banners, glass, paraments, and other places. Assign one or two symbols to small groups. Give learners an index card for each symbol so they can record where they find them. After providing enough search time, invite learners to return to the font and share where they found symbols.

The Service of Baptism

Invite learners to sit in the pews or chairs and look through the hymnal to find the service for baptism. Ask volunteers to read all the parts of this service, pausing to explain sections, ask questions, and point out symbols. Ask a family from the congregation to visit your group during this time and talk about the baptism of their infant. Provide time for learners to ask questions.

Baptism Booklet

Distribute Reproducible Page C, glue sticks, scissors, and markers or pencils. Guide learners to coloring, cutting out, and folding the half of the page that contains three panels. Then tell learners to cut out the eight squares to make a Baptism Booklet. Cut construction paper into five 4" x 11" (10 cm x 28 cm) strips, stack the strips, and fold them in half to make a booklet. Use a stapler or tie string around the fold to keep pages together. Learners can glue the squares on the left pages and draw or write on the right pages. Learners can decorate their booklets with symbols.

Closing Prayer

Dear Lord, thank you for welcoming us into your family through baptism. Wash us clean of our sins so we can live a new life. Amen

Learner Goals

KNOW
Bible stories about baptism

GROW
in understanding how baptism brings them into God's family

SHOW
recognition of baptismal symbols

Teacher Prayer

Dear God, thank you for your parental love and for making us a part of your family through baptism. Help us to keep your family harmonious and loving. Amen

Question for Reflection

What symbols, sounds, or words remind you of your own baptism?

Getting Ready for Jesus

Bible Text

John 1:1-18

Key Verse

In the beginning was the Word, and the Word was with God, and the Word was God. John 1:1

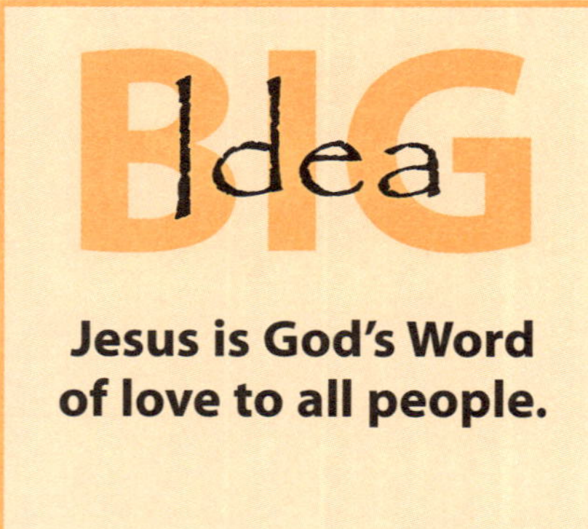

M&P

READY FOR THE STORY

Holiday decorations like garlands, wreaths, tinsel, and ribbon; birthday decorations like streamers, party hats, and signs; drawing paper, markers

Bible Background

The Gospel of John celebrates the incarnation. God's divine Word becomes flesh. The mystery of Jesus is that he is both human and divine, earthly and heavenly, mortal and eternal. This Gospel was written "so that you may come to believe that Jesus is the Messiah, the Son of God, and that through believing you may have life in his name" (John 20:31). Believers are beckoned to partake of the divine life Jesus brings to us.

As God spoke the cosmos into being (Genesis 1), again God speaks and God's Word becomes flesh. That Word—Jesus—is God's self-expression. That Word—Jesus—is eternal and always with God and, at the same time, coming into the world, into history, with us. That Word—Jesus—is the true light and enlightens everyone. By him, believers may witness and share in the divine life as God's own children born of God.

John, too, was sent from God as a witness to what he had not yet seen. None of us has seen God, which might make believing in God hard, except that God's Word in the human Jesus makes God known.

In the ancient Greek world God and human, spirit and flesh, and heaven and earth were sharply divided. In Jesus we meet God and human in one, signaling God's reconciliation with human beings. God's redemption in Jesus Christ reunites spirit and flesh. Heaven and earth meet in Jesus. We can live together with God.

Ready for the Story (10 minutes)

After greeting learners by name, ask them to decorate the room with holiday and birthday decorations. When all learners have arrived, remind learners that we celebrate the birth of Jesus at Christmas. Invite each learner to make a birthday card for Jesus. Display the cards in your classroom.

Explore the Story (25 minutes)

Pass out Bibles and ask learners to turn to the Gospel of John. **What Christian holiday is coming soon?** *(Christmas.)* **The Gospel of John tells the Christmas story in a different way. Instead of telling us about baby Jesus lying in a manger, this story tells us that Jesus is "the Word." Let's read John's Christmas story. Listen for each time this story says "the Word."** Ask a volunteer to read John 1:1-18. Then ask another volunteer to reread the passage, stopping just before every "the Word." When the reader stops, lead the class in substituting the word "Jesus" in place of "the Word." **What other words do we hear in this story?** *(Light, world, flesh.)*

Distribute magazines and ask learners to find examples of famous athletes, musicians, and actors who represent companies that sell products like cars, soft drinks, and shoes. Ask learners to think of other examples. **These people are**

called spokesmen or spokeswomen because they speak words for the company. What messages do they send about these products? Why do people believe what they say? *(Accept learner responses.)* **In this Bible story, we hear Jesus called "the Word." What do you think this means?** *(Accept learner responses.)* **Jesus was like a spokesman, or messenger, for God. What message did Jesus spread? Why do people believe Jesus?** *(Accept learner responses.)* **When Jesus lived on earth, he told people how much God loves them. He also showed us how to live together peacefully and help other people. If Jesus was a spokesman today, what words do you think he would say?** Invite learners to create ads and come up with slogans that spread Jesus' message. Display these words in the classroom.

Live the Story (25 minutes)

After completing both activities, finish the session with the Closing Prayer. Distribute copies of Reproducible Sheet Q and encourage them to make Advent wreaths at home with their families.

Gather Around the Wreath

Place four purple or blue candles, one white candle, and several silk or natural evergreen boughs in front of learners. **In church and in many Christian homes, we use an Advent wreath. The wreath can help us have patience and wait for Jesus' birth. I will show you how to make one.** Point to the greenery. **The base with green leaves reminds us of new life that we have in Jesus.** Arrange the greenery in a circle. **For an Advent wreath, we place candles in a circle. Circles are like God's love for us—they never end!** Put the four blue or purple candles along the outside of the wreath. **The four candles on the outside are blue or purple. Those are royal colors our church uses to represent Advent.** Read about each of the four candles on Reproducible Sheet Q. Place the white candle in the middle of the wreath. **We light the Christ candle in the middle on Christmas Eve. It is white to remind us that Jesus is the light of the world.** Read the prophecy in Isaiah 9:6. Light the appropriate number of candles. (Before lighting candles, check your local fire codes and your congregations fire policies regarding the use of open flames.) Ask learners to look at Reproducible Page B. **The four candles on the outside of the Advent wreath are symbols for hope, peace, joy, and love. Let's think of some pictures, or symbols, that show these things.** Help learners think of symbols to draw in the four boxes on the page. Symbols could include flames, rainbows, green leaves, peace signs, smiles, suns, and hearts.

Spread the Word

Distribute boxes, index cards, wrapping paper, tape, and scissors to learners. **We will prepare gifts for family and friends, but instead of buying presents, we can give them words about Jesus.** Learners can copy a verse from John 1:1-18 on an index card, decorate the card, place the card in a box, and wrap it.

Closing Prayer

Loving God, thank you for sending Jesus as your Word of love. Help us to prepare for the birth of Jesus. Amen

M&P

EXPLORE THE STORY
Bibles, kid-friendly magazines, paper, markers, pencils

LIVE THE STORY
Copies of Reproducible Page B (page 00 in Teacher Guide) and Reproducible Sheet Q (TCK), Bibles, natural or silk evergreen boughs, four blue or purple candles, one white candle, matches or lighter, small boxes, wrapping paper, scissors, tape, markers or crayons, and index cards

Learner Goals

KNOW
Jesus is the Word

GROW
in understanding Advent as a time of patience and waiting

SHOW
generosity to others by preparing gifts of words

Teacher Prayer

Dear Jesus, thank you for coming as a baby and living with us in human form. In these hurried days, give us patience and help us understand the true meaning of the Christmas season. Amen

Question for Reflection

What message, or "Word," does Jesus say to you?

The Lord's Prayer

Bible Text

Luke 11:1-13

Key Verse

[Jesus] said to them, "When you pray, say: 'Father, hallowed be your name. Your kingdom come. [Jesus also said] "Ask, and it will be given you; search, and you will find; knock and the door will be opened for you." Luke 11:2, 9

Jesus teaches us how to pray.

READY FOR THE STORY

Large paper for signs, index cards, crayons or markers, tape or tacky wall adhesive

Bible Background

The Bible frequently tells of Jesus praying. Increasingly surrounded by people eager to hear him, Jesus sometimes went alone to pray (Luke 5:16; 9:18). Having engaged in controversies and conflicts with the religious leaders, Jesus might pray through the night (Luke 6:12). Jesus prayed with others as part of corporate worship and he prayed with his disciples (Luke 9:28). As Jesus was facing his death, he prayed (Luke 22:41-42). Jesus prayed from the cross (Luke 23:34). Jesus' final words were words of prayer (Luke 23:46). Seeing that prayer was such an important part of Jesus' life, it's not surprising that his disciples asked him to teach them to pray.

Jesus' response to the disciples has four parts. Jesus teaches them a specific prayer (verses 2-4). Jesus teaches the importance of persistence in prayer by comparing how God responds to their prayers to how a friend might respond even to an inconvenient request (verses 5-8). Jesus teaches by giving words of encouragement to pray—ask, search, knock—and reassurance that prayers receive responses (verses 9-10). Jesus teaches that God's response to their needs expressed in prayer is like a good parent's response to a child's needs (verses 11-13). The Bible has two versions of the Lord's Prayer (Luke 11:2-4; Matthew 6:9-13). Ancient manuscripts have additional variations. Protestant church traditions add a doxology, words giving glory to God, which are based on David's prayer in 1 Chronicles 29:11-13.

When we talk and listen to God in prayer, we acknowledge that God is a friend who is ready not only to listen to our prayers, but also to respond. Practice helps us know that we can always go to God with the words and feelings of our hearts and minds. The prayer Jesus taught gives us words to use alone or with others. (Notice, though, that the prayer uses "us," "our," and "we," drawing us to one another as well as to God.) We can use the Lord's Prayer anytime, perhaps especially when we aren't sure what to pray or can't find words to express what we want to say. Jesus encourages us both to persist in prayer and to trust God's loving response.

Ready for the Story (10 minutes)

Before learners arrive, tape three signs to three parts of the wall. The signs should say *People, The World Around Me,* and *Thanks*. As learners arrive, greet them by name and give them a few index cards. Ask them to write or draw people they know, a situation in their community or broader world, and something they're thankful for. Once they're done drawing or writing, ask them to put the cards under the corresponding signs. **Today we will talk about prayer. Prayer is how we communicate with God, any time, anywhere. We can pray for everything you wrote or drew. Let's talk about how we could pray for these people and situations.** Discuss what learners wrote and drew on the cards. Tell learners you will include these requests during the prayer at the end of the session.

Explore the Story (35 minutes)

Distribute Bibles, hymnals, and Reproducible Page E to learners. **Sometimes it's hard to pray. We may feel like we don't know what to pray for, or like we're praying the wrong way. Even Jesus' disciples needed some help! They saw Jesus praying very often, so they asked Jesus to teach them how to pray.** Tell learners to turn to Luke 11 in their Bibles. Ask a volunteer to read the first two verses and tell the group to join in when they recognize the words. Stop after verse 4. **Is this the whole Lord's Prayer as we use it today?** *(No.)* **The prayer in the Bible is shorter.** Direct learners to open their hymnals to the Lord's Prayer in the worship service. Compare and contrast the two versions. **When you are baptized, your family and sponsors promise to teach you the Lord's Prayer.** Guide learners through "The Lord's Prayer: In Your Words" on Reproducible Page E.

After these verses that teach us the Lord's Prayer, Jesus tells us why it is important to keep praying to God. Ask a volunteer to read Luke 11:9-10. **Jesus tells us to ask, search, and knock. It's easy to remember these three words because their first letters spell ASK.** Ask volunteers to read "The Power of Prayer." After talking about Tim's story, share a time in your life when you have seen the power of prayer. Encourage learners to share other stories of successful prayer. Some may say they have prayed but were disappointed with the outcome. **God answers prayer, but sometimes we have to wait a long time, or the answer is not what we expect. The important thing is to talk to God and trust God for guidance so that we are thinking about what God wants us to do.**

Review the prayer cards posted under the signs. Talk about different ways to pray for each concern. For example, if a learner wrote the name of sibling, talk about how we could praise God for families, ask for God to help us get along, or tell God we are sorry for hurting them. Learners can write their prayer concerns in "A Personal Prayer."

Live the Story (15 minutes)

Prayer Cards

Ask your pastor for names and addresses of people in the congregation who need healing and wellness. Distribute cardstock and markers. Share the names of these congregational members in need of prayer. Invite learners to say a prayer for this person and then write a card of encouragement. After learners address the cards, send them to the members.

One-Word Prayers

Distribute construction paper so learners can trace their hands and cut out the hands. Ask learners to think of one word that describes a prayer concern. The word could be a person's name, a place, or a concept. After writing their single-word prayers on the hands, learners can glue hands to the posterboard. Ask learners to think of a title for their prayer collage.

Closing Prayer

After completing both activities, finish the session by praying for the concerns learners wrote on the index cards at the beginning of the session. Close with the Lord's Prayer. Distribute copies of Reproducible Sheet R and encourage learners to talk about prayer at home with their families.

M&P

EXPLORE THE STORY
Copies of Reproducible Page E (page 00 in Teacher Guide), Bibles, hymnals, dictionaries, pencils or markers

LIVE THE STORY
Copies of Reproducible Sheet E, cardstock, envelopes, and markers for "Prayer Cards"; poster board, construction paper, scissors, and markers for "One-Word Prayers"

Learner Goals

KNOW
how to pray the Lord's Prayer

GROW
in their understanding of how Jesus taught us to pray

SHOW
concern for others in their prayers

Teacher Prayer

Loving God, be with all children as they learn to talk with you through prayer. Help me grow in my own prayer life. Thank you for listening to and answering my prayers. In your holy name I pray, Amen

Question for Reflection

How do you listen for God's response to your prayers?

Christian Connections

DeVINE Crossword

■	1	■	■	2 J		3		■
4 G					■		■	■
■		■	■	5			6 D	
■	■	■	■		■	■		■
7 G		8		S				E
	■		■		■	■		■
	■	S	■	9	10	11		
	■		■	12 M				■
13			■		■	■	■	■
	■	14 N		V		15	■	16 E
■	17	■	■		■	18		
■	19 C						■	
■		■	■		■	20 S		

Across
2. disciple of Jesus
4. fruit in a vineyard
5. baby plants
7. Bible teaching…
9. "Let your light _ _ _ _ _."
12. belonging to me
13. A bird hatches from an _ _ _.
14. new and different; a storybook
18. last stage
19. hangs on to
20. Jesus is God's _ _ _.

Down
1. limb of a person
2. Bible teaching…
3. garden tool
6. heavenly; God-like
7. where flowers, fruit, and vegetables grow
8. God's plan is a good _ _ s _ _ n
10. Hello!
11. not out
15. fewer
16. God's first garden
17. do something

DeVINE Rap

Perform this rap in 4/4 time. Then teach it to friends or someone in your family!

Refrain:
Jesus is our master, our leader deVINE. *(make sign of cross on chest)*
We are the branches on Jesus' vine! *(reach out)*

God is our gardener in heaven *(point up)*, on earth *(point down)*.
Who planted his seed here *(planting motions)*, at Jesus' birth
(rock baby). *(Refrain)*

Because we all cling to Jesus' vine *(arms around chest)*,
We'll all bear the fruit of God's design! *(hands out) (Refrain)*

We'll always follow Jesus in all we do *(walk 4 steps to right in time to rap)*.
We'll share the love of Jesus *(hand over heart)*
with you and you! *(point at others) (Refrain)*

Vineyard Words

How many words can you make from the letters in VINEYARD?

____

____

____

____

____

____

____

Bread of Life

Whiny Travelers

Retell this story from Exodus 16 about the Israelites traveling to the promised land. After the leader reads each sentence in bold, everyone can repeat the sentence while doing the motions.

Going to the promised land.	Make walking movements.
Coming to the Red Sea.	Stop walking.
God parts the Red Sea.	Make pushing movements with arms.
Crossing the dry sea.	Make walking movements again.
Walking in the hot, dry, empty desert.	Make walking movements and wipe forehead.
Walking through the sand.	Pretend to trudge through heavy sand.
We're getting tired!	Make a whiny face.
We're getting thirsty!	Make a whiny face and point to throat.
We're getting hungry!	Make a whiny face and point to stomach.
We should have stayed in Egypt!	Make a whiny face and point behind you.
At least we had food in Egypt!	Put hands on hips.
Look! Our leader, Moses, is praying to God!	Make praying hands.
Maybe we'll get something to eat!	Look hopeful.
Moses says God will send us meat and bread!	Look happy and excited.
Look! Here comes a big flock of quail!	Look toward the sky.
Yummy quail to eat!	Pat stomach.
Let's go to sleep.	Close eyes and pretend to sleep.
Morning is here.	Open eyes and stretch.
Look! What's that pearly stuff?	Jump up and place hand above eyes to look.
Moses says it's manna, God's bread!	Pat stomach.
Let's make manna pancakes! Hooray!	Show your joy about having food!

Bread of Life Banquet

Jesus often went to friends' homes for dinner. Suppose you learn that Jesus will come to your Sunday school class next week. Your group wants to entertain and feed him. How would you prepare? Use this checklist to plan food, decorations, entertainment, and activities at your Bread of Life banquet!

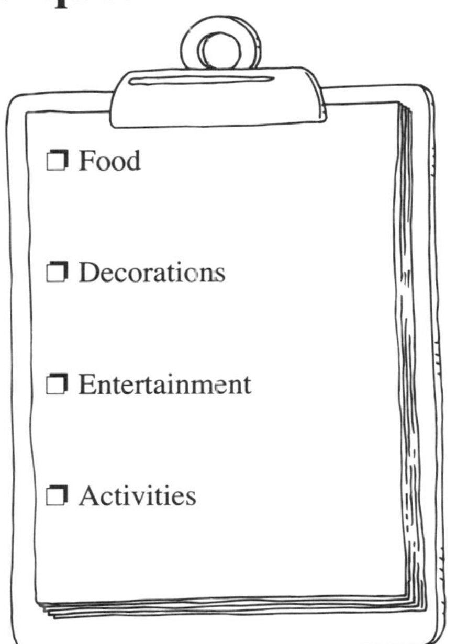

The Sacrament of Baptism

Joining God's Family

Color these pictures and cut on the solid line. Fold between the pictures on the dotted lines so that they will stand up. Tell a friend about baptism!

My Own Baptism

Cut out each of these squares. Glue each one to a page in your Baptism Booklet. Leave room on the other side of the page to answer the questions.

What did you wear at your baptism?	Who attended your baptism? Family members, friends, people in your church family?	Did the congregation present you with any gifts? What were they?	What happened during your baptism service?
Did you cry when the pastor poured water on you, or were you asleep?	Where is your baptismal certificate?	What does the certificate say?	Have you seen anyone else's baptism? What happened?

Getting Ready for Jesus

Jesus Brings Many Gifts

As you celebrate Advent, think about the gifts that Jesus brings us: Hope, Peace, Joy, and Love. Draw a symbol for each of these gifts.

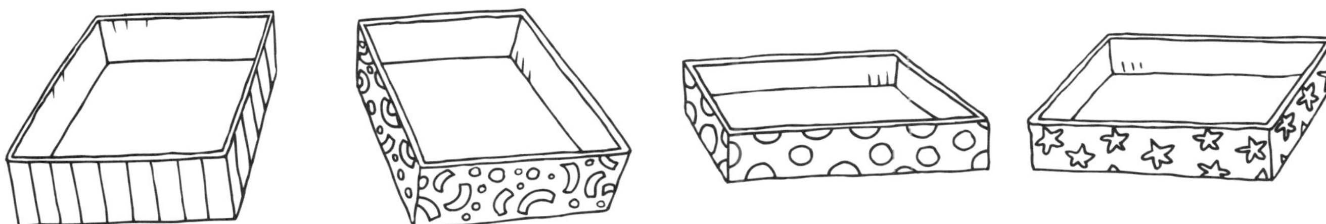

There are four weeks to get ready for Jesus' birthday. Each week before Christmas, think about a way you can share these gifts from Jesus with others.

Week 1: Hope

- If there is a negative story on TV, say a prayer of hope.
- When you see a baby, hope for the baby's future.
- Tell your teacher or another adult about something that you hope for them.
- Look up the word *hope* in the dictionary. What does it say?

Week 2: Peace

- If you are mad at someone, count to 10 and take 3 deep breaths instead of fighting back.
- Put your finger somewhere on a world map and pray for peace in that place.
- When you see your friends, make a peace sign.
- Look up the word *peace* in the dictionary. What does it say?

Week 3: Joy

- Wear a pin or sticker with a smiling face.
- Ask adult family members to describe a joyful day in their lives.
- Try to laugh with your friends for a whole minute.
- Look up the word *joy* in the dictionary. What does it say?

Week 4: Love

- Surprise your family by making early valentines.
- Find a Bible verse that talks about love, and make a bookmark or magnet of it.
- If you know someone who speaks another language, ask how to say love in that language.
- Look up the word *love* in the dictionary. What does it say?

The Lord's Prayer

The Lord's Prayer In Your Words

Jesus taught us to pray like this.

Our Father in **heaven**,
hallowed be your name.
your **kingdom** come,
your **will** be done
on **earth** as in heaven.
Give us today our daily **bread**.
Forgive us our sins,
as we **forgive** those
who **sin** against us.
Save us from the time of **trial**
and **deliver** us from **evil**.
For the kingdom, the **power**,
and the **glory** are yours,
now and **forever**. Amen

Look up each bold word in the dictionary. Write down one or two synonyms, or words that mean the same thing. Choose one of these words to put in the blank, and read the prayer again. How does it sound now?

Our Father in ______________,
______________ be your name.
your ______________ come,
your ______________ be done
on ______________ as in heaven.
Give us today our daily ______________.
______________ us our sins,
as we ______________ those
who ______________ against us.
______________ us from the time of ______________
and ______________ us from ______________
For the kingdom, the ______________,
and the ______________ are yours,
now and ______________. Amen

The Power of Prayer

Read this true story about a boy named Tim.
Then share a time when God answered your prayer.

Tim was a little older than you, but he enjoyed many of the same activities. He liked to run, swim, play sports, and go places with his friends. Tim enjoyed his church youth group.

One summer, he joined his friends on a bus trip to a church camp. While they were on the road, there was a terrible accident. The bus flipped over, and Tim was thrown out of the bus. Several of his friends were killed, and Tim was rushed to the hospital. He had many broken bones, and the blood was no longer flowing into one hip. The doctors told him he'd never walk or play sports again, even after many operations.

Tim was very sad, but he was also courageous. He began to pray. His parents and grandmother prayed, and everyone they knew prayed, too! Tim's grandmother even put Tim on an Internet prayer chain.

Then a miracle happened. Tim returned to the doctor, who was amazed to find that Tim's hip, which had been so broken up, was healing! Now Tim is learning to walk again. He won't need surgery after all. Tim will have to remain courageous and work very hard to recover, but God is healing him! Tim now expects to be able to run and play sports like he used to. God has answered his prayers and the prayers that other people prayed on his behalf.

A Personal Prayer

Make up your own prayer, using these suggestions.

Praise God.
Ask God to help you with something.
Ask God to forgive you.
Thank God.